EASY TECH:
CASES AND MATERIALS ON
COURTROOM TECHNOLOGY

NATIONAL INSTITUTE FOR TRIAL ADVOCACY

EASY TECH:
CASES AND MATERIALS ON
COURTROOM TECHNOLOGY

Frank D. Rothschild
Deanne C. Siemer
Anthony J. Bocchino

Contributing Authors

**Donald H. Beskind, Kenneth S. Broun,
Richard M. Markus, James R. Seckinger, Edward R. Stein**

© 2001 by the National Institute for Trial Advocacy

Rothschild, Frank D., Deanne C. Siemer, Anthony J. Bocchino, *Easy Tech: Cases and Materials on Courtroom Technology* (NITA, 2001).

FBA715-0

5/01

Table of Contents

Acknowledgments

The authors would like to thank the following for their assistance in the creation of the video clips that come with these files: Nancy and Scott Lindman (Roberta Quinlan and Brian Kane), both realtors and golfing partners in real life; Heidi Rodgers, Esq. (examining attorney for Quinlan and Byrd); Brian Kennelly (examining attorney for Quinlan and Byrd); Beau Williams (James Lawrence), he does lawn and yard work in real life, too, but has never snatched a purse—or so he says; Lisa Breen (Gale Fitzgerald), organic farmer; Eric Lutz (Ken Brown), tennis pro at Hanalei Bay Resort in real life; Sam Jajich, Esq. (Robert Byrd).

How to Use the CD-ROM

This book includes a CD-ROM that contains PowerPoint® slide shows, digital copies of exhibits, and video clips for each of the three sample cases used to present basic concepts in the use of courtroom technology. Those who are familiar with the use of CDs as file storage media do not need to read this section, as this CD is standard in all respects. Those who are new to the use of CDs should review and follow these instructions.

This CD can be used in three ways—to examine the files that it contains; to work with these files by editing, supplementing, or copying them; and to display files for third persons in an office, classroom, or courtroom setting. If you are just perusing the files, you can use them efficiently on the CD. If you are working with or displaying the files for others, you will want to copy them to the hard drive of your computer so that they will play more quickly and smoothly. Each method is explained below.

TO VIEW THE FILES ON THE CD

1. Insert the CD into the CD drive of your computer.

2. Go to the Windows Desktop. This is the screen display that contains the icons for basic Windows functions as well as for software programs that have been installed on the computer.

3. Double click on the My Computer icon, which looks like this.

   This displays icons for each of the drives on your computer (usually A, C, D, and so on) together with some other basic controls. You are going to use the icon for the CD drive.

   Wait for a few seconds while the computer identifies the CD. It will change to show that it can read the disk by displaying a name under the icon like this.

   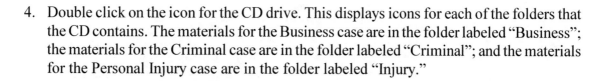

4. Double click on the icon for the CD drive. This displays icons for each of the folders that the CD contains. The materials for the Business case are in the folder labeled "Business"; the materials for the Criminal case are in the folder labeled "Criminal"; and the materials for the Personal Injury case are in the folder labeled "Injury."

5. Double click on the icon for the case that you want. This displays another series of folders labeled Part I, Part 2, Part 3, Exhibit Scans, and a PowerPoint icon, plus a number of video clip icons. In the Criminal case file, there is also a folder labeled "Problem 17."

6. To run the PowerPoint slide show for a case, first double click on the folder labeled Business, Criminal, or Injury case, then double click on the PowerPoint file with the extension .ppt that is inside the folder.

   PowerPoint will open the slide show automatically and then stop, waiting for further instructions.

7. Click on the Slide Show icon on the bottom left of the screen to go into "play mode." This is the set of instructions under which PowerPoint will go from one slide to the next so that you can look at all the slides in the collection. The screen display looks like this.

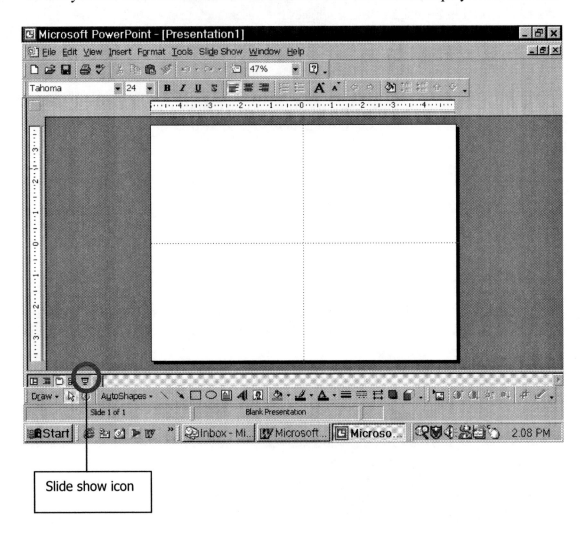

The first slide of the presentation will appear, which will be a blank slide in all one color.

- To display any other slide in the slide show, simply type the slide number (**NOT** the exhibit number) as shown in the thumbnail printouts at the back of each case file and hit the "Enter" key.

- To see the next slide in order, click the left mouse or press the space bar.

- To go back one slide, press the "Page Up" key.

- To go to any other slide, type the slide number and hit the Enter key.

- To play animations (if the slide contains any), either left click the mouse or press the space bar to initiate each animation.

- To take projected images off the screen or monitor and go back to a neutral blank screen, type in "1" plus "Enter" to return to the first slide.

- To play the video clips, bring up the slide you want by typing the slide number and hitting "Enter," then move the mouse cursor into the image [you might need to move the mouse around rapidly for a second or two to see the cursor on the screen]. Once in the video image, the cursor will change from a pointed arrow into a little white hand. That is your signal that the video is ready to play. Left click once and the video will play. You can stop and start the video with a left mouse click so long as the cursor remains inside the image.

- To display Q & A text in synch with a video, start the video (as above), then put the cursor outside the image [it will change back to an arrow] and click the left mouse to bring up each Q & A in synch with the video. It is simple and takes little practice to master.

TO TRANSFER THE FILES TO YOUR COMPUTER'S HARD DRIVE

For best results, it is highly recommended that you download the files from the CD to your hard drive. The slide shows and video clips will play faster and much more smoothly this way. The easiest way to accomplish this is as follows.

1. Open the CD in My Computer.

2. Click on Edit on the top toolbar.

3. From the drop-down menu, click "Select All," which will highlight all of the folders on the CD.

4. Right click on those selected folders.

5. Select the "Send to" option and, from that menu, click on "My Documents." the folders will be copied to your hard drive in the My Documents folder.

To answer other questions you may have, please refer to *PowerPoint for Litigators*, Siemer, Rothschild, Stein, and Solomon (NITA, 2000).

Introduction

This book is designed to facilitate the teaching of evidence presentation technology without complicated fact patterns or expensive equipment. The problems are drawn from common courtroom situations, and the exercises using these problems build skills that are relevant to most specialties within trial practice. Thinking about the visual aspects of presenting a case is also directly relevant to arbitration, mediation, and other forms of alternative dispute resolution.

The exercises are devoted to the most common presentation technology:

- the evidence camera and projector (also known as a document camera, a visualizer, a visual presenter, an Elmo, or a Doar Presenter)
- the laptop computer and projector
- the telestrator (also known as the "John Madden pen" or illustrator).

There are many varieties of equipment sets, wiring methods, displays, and enhancements that may be used for presentations in court. Some courtrooms are fully equipped; others require lawyers to bring in their own equipment. The basic methods taught with the materials in this book are appropriate in most trial situations. Once the basics are mastered, more specialized equipment and more esoteric methods are easily incorporated into the student's arsenal.

Three small case files present facts that can be mastered quickly:

- a contract case, *Quinlan v. Kane*
- a criminal case, *State v. Lawrence*
- a personal injury case, *Brown v. Byrd*

Each case supports exercises in direct and cross-examination, opening statements, and closing argument so that the basic work of a trial lawyer is covered. Each case file has six parts: (1) a summary of facts; (2) jury instructions; (3) the verdict form; (4) deposition summaries, including transcript excerpts from the videotape of the deposition; (5) copies of the exhibits; and (6) problems. The printed materials are supplemented by a CD that contains digital versions of each of the exhibits and videotapes, together with typical visual displays that would be used by each side to present the case.

The case files in this book are designed to facilitate teaching students how to use two kinds of courtroom displays:

- Evidentiary exhibits, which are enlargements of exhibits or parts of exhibits that are admitted in evidence, so that the content of the exhibit can be more easily followed during testimony; and

- Illustrative aids, which are enhancements of exhibits (through labels, highlighting, callouts) and materials specially prepared for litigation (such as bullet point slides, or charts or diagrams) that are used to assist in the explanation of the testimony but are not admitted in evidence.

Easy Tech: Cases and Materials on Courtroom Technology
© The National Institute for Trial Advocacy

Typically, exhibits may go to the jury room when the jury retires to deliberate, but illustrative aids are not allowed to go to the jury room. There is always some confusion about this because both evidentiary exhibits and illustrative aids are given exhibit numbers and may be mixed together in the same numbering series. Students should differentiate these two types of exhibits and make a clear record.

Thoughtful use of visual material, coupled with clear oral statements, helps the fact finder move expeditiously through the case with a good understanding of the facts. It is not necessary to know how to prepare the visual aids themselves in order to use them well. However, it is necessary to master the presentation techniques in order to get visual material before the fact finder in an effective manner. Presentation technology helps make points effectively, but does not substitute for a persuasive case theory. In order to focus on the presentation techniques, each case file supplies guidance about one plausible case theory and a sample of the visual materials that might be used by each side. Students are encouraged to develop alternative theories as time allows.

Formulating and stating objections also changes as more visual material is introduced in the courtroom, whether as evidentiary exhibits or as illustrative aids. The traditional oral cues that prompt an objection on hearsay or undue prejudice grounds, for example, give way to visual cues such as words in a label, unfair cropping of a document, or distortion of a photo. Just as the advocate needs to know what to listen for when the stream of information is oral, he or she needs to know what to look for when the information is delivered visually.

Presentation technology is a generic term for anything used in a courtroom (or arbitration hearing room) to display exhibits electronically or digitally. The use of this technology began in the 1970s when slide projectors, overhead projectors, and videotape players made an appearance in courtrooms. They were followed in the early 1980s by the more sophisticated laser disk players that did the same work but more reliably and with better quality. In the early 1990s, CD-ROM players offered more versatility, evidence cameras were often seen in big trials, and telestrator units helped by providing the capability to "draw" on the computer screen. In the mid-1990s, the laptop computer gradually began to supplant much that had gone before it and, with the most recent boosts in chip capacity, the laptop can now do almost all of the courtroom tasks involved in the presentation of exhibits. Everything lawyers use as exhibits—photos, documents, lists, quotes, transcripts, video clips, maps, diagrams, drawings, time lines, graphs, relationship charts, spreadsheets, organizational charts—can now be created, ordered, animated, and projected with surprising ease, and at a fraction of the cost of older methods.

As laptop computers were adding enormous amounts of capacity, digital projectors began to lose weight, increase in power, and operate well in fully lighted rooms. Because many courtrooms have nothing friendlier to presentation technology than an electrical outlet, these small, lightweight, reliable projectors quickly became mainstream equipment for courtroom use. Similarly, ten-foot projection screens began appearing that are easy to set up, quickly dismantled, and well suited to displaying exhibits. Some have better light enhancing surfaces that produce sharp images.

Flat panel computer monitors first appeared in small sizes in jury boxes and gradually became available in very large sizes suitable for viewing by the entire courtroom. Many courtrooms that have equipped themselves with presentation technology use monitors instead of projection screens. This book uses projection screens as the model as this is the most inexpensive and widely available equipment.

The laptop computer solved most of the problems inherent in older methods. The blackboard presents a near impossibility of adequately preserving for the record what was drawn on it. A computer preserves a precise record of every action. Hand drawn flip charts are sometimes hard to read and favor the lawyer with good handwriting and an eye for perspective in drawing. A computer provides clear type and elegant design capabilities. Document blowups and photographic enlargements are time-consuming and expensive to create; and once completed, they cannot be changed. A computer can produce blowups and enlargements virtually cost-free with the flexibility to change at any time.

The lightweight, high powered digital projectors also solved a principal problem with earlier technology. Slide projectors and overhead projectors require dimming of the lights in the courtroom. Newer digital projectors that take images from a computer have the projection strength to work well in full daylight.

A lawyer with a laptop can walk up, plug in, and the display monitors or screens all light up with presentations driven by the computer. When this happens, the advocate with the technology-enhanced displays often has a significant advantage in holding jurors' attention and creating a faster understanding of the facts, themes, and images that drive the case. This also means that advocates perhaps not as oratorically gifted as their opponents but armed with this technology, can level the playing field of persuasion. The images on the screen speak for themselves.

Courtroom visuals help the finder of fact to grasp the overall theme, absorb the important details of the case, and learn the relationships among facts far more readily than can be accomplished by speech alone. When people listen to a trial lawyer explain something new, they try to picture it in their minds. Using a visual display ensures that listeners will have a good opportunity to form the same mental pictures of the facts as the lawyer has. Visuals motivate people to pay more attention, and they make understanding easier. For a well-prepared lawyer, the advantage gained by adding visual displays is almost always substantial, no matter what kind of case is being litigated. If your opponent uses visuals effectively, that is an advantage you cannot afford to give away.

PART I: PROBLEMS IN BASIC PRESENTATION TECHNOLOGY

Three types of presentation technology account for most of the current usage in federal and state courts and will continue to dominate in the future. An understanding of when, where, and how to use these technologies can increase the advocate's effectiveness in almost any kind of case. This part describes each method and sets out exercises that will familiarize you with the operation of the equipment.

1.   THE EVIDENCE CAMERA AND PROJECTOR

The evidence camera consists of a small TV camera mounted on a retractable arm connected to a light box that serves as a base. The base is connected via cable to a projector. When plugged in and connected by cable, the evidence camera will display an image of anything that is placed under or in front of it. It has the capability to zoom in to enlarge the image of items not easily displayed otherwise. It is also known as a "document camera" (although it is actually not very good at displaying many types of documents), a "visualizer" and a "visual presenter." Its most common commercial names are the "Elmo" and the "Doar Presenter."

The evidence camera enhances the lawyer's presentation by focusing everyone in the courtroom on the point being explained. Everyone is on the same page, so to speak, as the lawyer proceeds. Other means can achieve this objective. Enlarged graphics on an easel, or transparencies on an overhead projector, also present details and focus attention, but the evidence camera is faster, more flexible, and more efficient.

The evidence camera is about eighteen inches square. It has no special mounting requirements. The unit will sit on any table or other level surface. The evidence camera unit has an AC plug outlet on the back panel. It is connected to a standard electrical outlet through a power strip to guard against unusual spikes in the electrical current.

The evidence camera travels well. It weighs about nine pounds, and folds up into a convenient carrying case. The arm that supports the camera head retracts (with a release button on the side of the arm) so that it fits within the footprint of the base. The arm also folds down (with a release button next to the point where the arm joins the base) to put the head on the surface of the base.

A.   Best uses

The evidence camera works best with material that, once enlarged sufficiently, is quite clear without much additional highlighting or other marking. The camera enlarges very well, but it does not support complicated additions to an enlarged exhibit. Its best uses are photos (and similar materials such as maps and drawings), small objects, and uncomplicated material from documents.

Photos

The evidence camera is an inexpensive and flexible way to enlarge photographs, particularly those in color. Any photo can be enlarged to the desired size using the focus and zoom capabilities of the evidence camera. For example, suppose the witness testifies that a particular railroad crossing is in a commercial area. The witness has several photos of the crossing used to support this conclusion. If the cross-examiner spots cows grazing in one tiny area in the upper left corner of the photo, the photo can be placed on the evidence camera base, the lawyer can zoom in until just the area featuring the cows occupies the entire display screen, and the cross-examination can proceed from there. The evidence camera produces the necessary enlargement instantly and electronically. A hard copy enlargement from the photo might take days to get and the resolution might not be as good.

Photos are the easiest exhibits to present using an evidence camera. Because they lie flat on the base, there are no problems with depth of field in adjusting the focus. Some photos are best presented simply by placing them on the base under the camera so that an enlarged version appears on the screen. No adjustments or other actions are required. The zoom-in feature, as explained below, works well with photos to highlight a particular portion of the scene.

X-rays, MRI images and CAT scans

The evidence camera does an excellent job of displaying x-rays, MRI images, and CAT scans. These exhibits need light pushed up from the base. The light in the base is turned on with an on/off switch located at the left front of the unit and labeled "BASE." The evidence camera has an iris adjustment knob, located on the camera head to get the best possible contrast for x-rays. The evidence camera also has a positive/negative switch, located on the front control panel, to provide flexibility in the way the image is displayed. X-rays can be shown either in "negative" (which is their normal state) or "positive." As a negative, the x-ray displays its subject on a black background. One normally receives information on a white background, and it is easier for jurors to understand the content of the x-ray when it is displayed this way. The positive/negative switch allows you to change from negative (white on black) to positive (black on white).

35 mm slides, regular film negatives, and other transparencies

The evidence camera will enlarge 35 mm slides to whatever size is needed. Simply put the slide on the base of the camera, turn on the base light, zoom in, and adjust the focus. Transparencies are displayed in the same manner. Regular negatives can be enlarged and turned into photos using the negative/positive switch. Put the negative on the base, turn the negative/positive switch to positive, and zoom in to the enlargement you need.

Small objects

Enlargement of small objects, such as a bullet, a computer chip, or a mechanical part, allows witnesses to testify about them while showing the "real thing" on the screen. Using the evidence camera, the object can be moved around to provide any necessary viewing angle for jury understanding of the testimony about the object. The lawyer or witness can pick up the object, rotate it on the evidence camera base so that a different side is showing, or turn it upside down. The camera will show on the screen all of these actions, so long as they are within its field of view. Relevant aspects of the object can be pointed out either by the witness standing next to the screen and indicating a location on the image or by the witness standing at the evidence camera and using a pointer directed at the object itself.

Simple document points

An enlarged display of words or small sections of text helps direct the jury's attention to the point to be extracted from a document. The evidence camera provides a limited capability to work with whole pages. Any display of the entire page reduces the text to a size too small to read. However, an enlarged display on the screen and the ability to interact with the document by highlighting it or pointing to a particular phrase help enhance a witness's testimony and make the evidence camera valuable in presenting simple document points.

Excerpts from books

The evidence camera allows you to show the entire book that your witness is using to bolster testimony, then turn to the section of the book in which the material you intend to emphasize is located, and finally to arrive at the page on which the material appears. The jury can follow this easily with the enlarged images on the screen.

Narrow columns

The evidence camera works best with text that is in narrow columns. The focus of the camera is limited to a span about five inches wide. Columns of about two inches, such as newspaper format, are ideal. The columns of condensed print on "minuscript" transcripts also work well on the evidence camera. Put the page down on the base under the camera. Use the zoom in feature to get to the particular text in which you are interested. You can now have the witness use the text working directly from the image on the screen while you point to it with your finger or pen.

B.   Operation

The operation of an evidence camera involves simply placing the evidence on the plate under the camera and operating the zoom button to get to the proper enlargement. The zoom feature on the evidence camera is like the zoom on a 35 mm camera or video camera. It allows the operator to change the focus of the lens to make the field of vision smaller and to enlarge every detail being

Easy Tech: Cases and Materials on Courtroom Technology
© The National Institute for Trial Advocacy

viewed. The controls are simple to operate. You press and hold down a button labeled "tele" until you get the amount of enlargement you want, and then take your finger off the button. To retreat from the enlargement and get back to normal size, you press another button labeled "wide" that changes the lens focus until you release the button. In nearly every case, the user will zoom in while the jury is watching and zoom out while nothing is being displayed and therefore the jury is not watching.

Zoom in

Zooming in is a natural action that is easily followed visually. The best technique for most exhibits is to show the whole exhibit for identification, zoom in to show a section of a photo, for example, and finish the point with the witness while the evidence camera remains zoomed in. In that way, the jury sees the exhibit as a whole and understands the context of the item on which you have zoomed in. For example, you might have an aerial photo of a city block. You want to show the group of buildings that were damaged when the city's water main broke. Start with the hard copy and have the witness identify it. Put the hard copy on the evidence camera and have the witness identify it again, preferably with its exhibit number showing. Ask the witness to point to the area where buildings were affected by the flood and to identify the cross streets. Now, zoom in on that point until the camera frames only the buildings about which you want the witness to talk.

To anchor yourself visually, when you put the photo down on the base, put your finger on the photo at a point a little below where you are going to finish up after you have zoomed in. Now, start zooming in. Watch the monitor, not the photo. Use your finger to move the photo so that the portion you want to feature is centered under the camera. This is more easily done than said. Your finger is the visual anchor, and you will not have to look down to see where you are going. Zoom the camera (focusing on a smaller and smaller area of the photo) and move the photo (gradually centering the area you want directly under the camera) at the same time. It is important not to move the photo after you have zoomed in. Do not zoom in randomly and then move the photo to get the zoom focused on the area where you want to be. The motion of the photo crossing under the camera creates a confusing visual effect and detracts from the exhibit. More important, you are likely to get disoriented and be unable to get back to the portion of the photo you want. If you make a mistake, it is better to back out a little, get oriented again, and then zoom back in.

After you take the photo off the base, and before you put down the next exhibit, press the "wide" button to zoom out. The evidence camera is now in its "base" position, and you are ready to zoom in again if the next exhibit calls for that action. Zooming out can be confusing and disorienting if an exhibit is under the camera. If you zoom in for one exhibit and forget to zoom out after you are finished with that exhibit, when you put the next exhibit on the base, the camera will be zoomed in on some very small portion of it. You will not get a smooth flow from one exhibit to the next because you will need to stop and zoom out to get the current exhibit into proper focus.

There are a few occasions when you might start with the evidence camera zoomed in and then zoom out to a broader view. For example, if you are trying to show a family relationship, you might start with the evidence camera zoomed in on an inset photo of the individual and then zoom out to show that individual's place in the family group or family tree. In a loss of consortium case, you might start zoomed in on the child alone and then zoom back to an extended family.

Easy Tech: Cases and Materials on Courtroom Technology
© The National Institute for Trial Advocacy

Zoom out can also be used to deal with photos that are out of context. Suppose that your opponent has a photo tightly focused on subject matter favorable to his case. You need to show that, in a wider context, that photo would show details favorable to your case. You could start in a zoomed in position with the photo, then put behind the photo a piece of paper containing a drawing or illustration of the missing details and zoom out to show the broader context. Zoom out can also occasionally be used with documents. If your opponent has focused on one or two words in the fine print, it may be useful to take the jury from those words back to the mass of fine print that faced the person who agreed to the insurance contract.

The other controls on the evidence camera are equally easy to master.

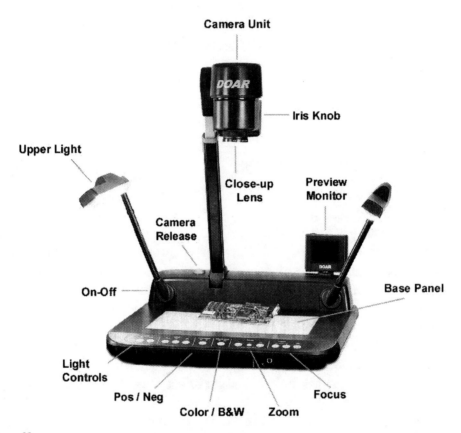

On-off

The evidence camera is an electronic device that needs to be plugged into a standard electrical outlet as a power source. When you plug it in and turn it on, the camera is activated. It stays activated until you turn it off or unplug it from the power source.

Aim

You aim the evidence camera in two basic ways. The standard "aim" is straight down, so that the camera is looking at whatever is placed on the base below it. Alternatively, the head can be turned to face outward, either to the front or the back, and in that position it will look at whatever is in front of it.

Easy Tech: Cases and Materials on Courtroom Technology
© The National Institute for Trial Advocacy

Lens and lens cap

The camera lens is protected by a lens cap which needs to be off when the unit is operating. The camera has a closeup lens which must be on when the camera is aimed down at its base. The closeup lens needs to be off in order for the unit to operate properly when the head is rotated to the front or back to focus on something at a distance.

Focus

Like any camera, the evidence camera needs to be focused in order to display a crisp, clear image. It has two focus controls, manual and automatic. The manual focus is operated by two buttons labeled "N" (near) and "F" (far). Manual focus is needed for any three-dimensional object because of the different depths of field presented by the object. The autofocus is operated by a single button located next to the manual focus buttons. Press it once, and it figures out where to focus. This is most useful with documents that lie flat on the base.

Iris knob

The iris control knob is located on the camera head. It darkens or lightens the image. Generally the setting is kept in the middle. The evidence camera has an auto iris that will adjust for the best contrast under most circumstances.

Light

The evidence camera works well in natural light. Most black and white exhibits need no additional light. For special exhibits, the evidence camera comes with two light sources. The arms above the base contain high intensity overhead lights that are turned on to help increase the contrast when you are presenting materials in color. The base contains a light that is turned on when you need light coming up through the material being presented—such as an x-ray or a transparency. Each set of lights (the one in the base and the ones in the arms) has a separate on/off switch. In normal operation, both sets of lights are off.

Black & white vs color switch

In normal operation, the black & white switch is on. The color switch activates an automated enhancement for color images. If the camera is aimed at something that has color in or on it, the color switch should be on. Color images can be turned to black and white by using the black & white switch also located on the control console.

Negative/positive switch

In normal operation, the negative/positive switch is set to positive. The negative switch is used with photographic negatives and x-rays when you want them to appear in their original condition and not as "positives."

Easy Tech: Cases and Materials on Courtroom Technology
© The National Institute for Trial Advocacy

C.   Setup

The most effective setup for an evidence camera in most courtrooms is to connect it to a digital projector which, in turn, displays images on a blank wall or a single large six, eight, or ten-foot screen. This makes relatively low demands on the technical skill of the person who does the courtroom setup. The cabling between the evidence camera and the projector is easy to connect, and the settings on the projector should be straightforward.

An evidence camera is an analog device. Its normal output is to a video monitor or video projector. It is not a digital device like a computer that outputs to a computer monitor or a digital projector. However, most newer model digital projectors have an on-board converter that takes input from an evidence camera.

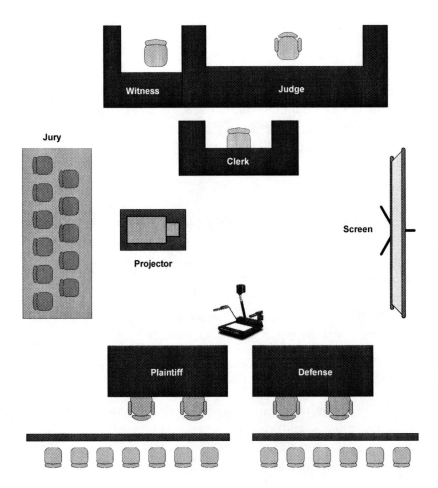

A projector demands considerable space in a courtroom. If possible, you want your screen located straight across from the jury box. You need about twice the distance from the first row of seats as the size of the screen. A six-foot screen will be about twelve feet from the audience; an eight-foot screen will be about sixteen feet away; and a ten-foot screen needs about twenty feet. Most experts think that the ten-foot screen is the best choice. The smaller screens do not produce the necessary visual impact. As a practical matter, you need a high ceiling and an area thirty-five to forty feet wide and forty to fifty feet deep to use a ten-foot screen effectively.

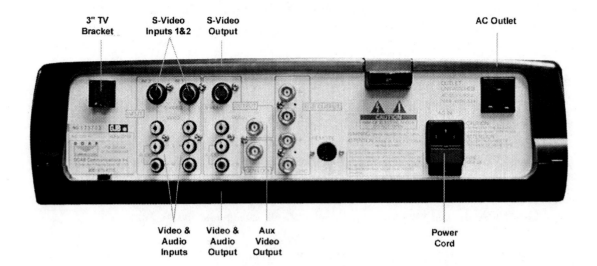

3" TV Bracket   S-Video Inputs 1&2   S-Video Output   AC Outlet

Video & Audio Inputs   Video & Audio Output   Aux Video Output   Power Cord

The evidence camera is cabled directly to the projector. This setup needs only two connections, one at either end of the cable. The evidence camera is putting OUT video signals to the projector where they are going to be displayed. Therefore, the cable from the evidence camera is connected to the evidence camera's jack labeled "line out." The projector is taking IN video signals from the evidence camera. Therefore the cable is connected to the projector's jack labeled "line in."

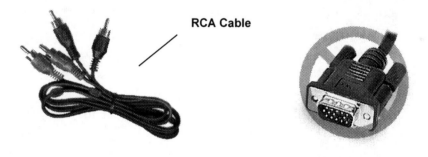

RCA Cable

The evidence camera needs RCA cable, which is the same cabling as used for hooking up a stereo. Computer cable will not work. The cable should be taped down so that no one trips over it. Gaffing tape (not duct tape) is useful for this as it does not leave a residue on the floor or carpet.

An evidence camera is a sturdy, simple unit that has excellent reliability. Once it is hooked up and operating, very few things can go wrong. The list below sets out the possibilities:

> Iris knob turned down: The camera has a control, called an iris knob, that adjusts the amount of light reaching the camera. If you accidentally turn the iris knob down, thus reducing the amount of light reaching the camera, the screen looks black. Turn the iris knob back up.

Closeup lens gone: There is a lens located at the aperture of the camera. If it is missing, the image projected will be out of focus. Put the lens back on.

Lens cover on: The camera lens has a cover to protect it when not in use. If you leave the lens cover on, no light will reach the camera. The screen will be black. Take the lens cover off.

Color switch off: If you are displaying an item that is black and white—such as a document that has only black type on white paper—the color switch should be off. This will produce a more crisp image. When you move to an item that is in color—such as a photo or chart—the color switch needs to be turned back on. Otherwise the colors on your exhibit will appear as shades of gray.

Bulb broken: If you drop the unit as you are running up the courthouse steps, you may break a bulb. Normally bulbs have a life of 2000 to 3000 hours, and they are not a problem in regular use. Make sure you have a spare.

Nonfunctioning electrical outlet: Courtroom electrical outlets may be non-functioning or only partially functioning. Sometimes courtroom maintenance is so poor that one after another outlet becomes nonfunctioning over the years until the entire courtroom is down to just one operational outlet. In some instances, outlets have been turned off for some purpose and never turned on again.

No converter on the projector: The evidence camera puts out analog signals. A digital projector uses digital signals. A converter is needed to change analog signals to digital signals. Most newer digital projectors have a converter on board and the evidence camera can be used with no special cabling. However, older models do not have on-board converters, and a converter (called a line doubler) must be put between the evidence camera and the projector. The evidence camera (output) is cabled to the line doubler (input), and the line doubler (output) is cabled to the projector (input).

D.   Techniques in using the evidence camera

The evidence camera's simple operation makes it a good choice for personal operation by the trial lawyer. When you pick up a document and put it down on the evidence camera base, the enlarged image of the document appears immediately on the screen. Judges and jurors see exactly how the operation works. When a lawyer says, "Directing your attention to the portion of this photograph above the first floor of the house," and puts the photo on the evidence camera base and presses the zoom button to bring an enlarged image of this area to the screen, the natural flow between the lawyer's words and the screen display enhances the appearance of competence and control.

The principal techniques for making the evidence presentation more effective with an evidence camera are set out below.

Easy Tech: Cases and Materials on Courtroom Technology
© The National Institute for Trial Advocacy

Identification

Normally it is not important for the jury to read the entire page of a document because you will be directing their attention to just a small portion of the page. When you put the page on the evidence camera base, focus for five seconds on something that reassures the jurors that this page is what you say it is. This may be the exhibit number in the lower right corner, the title, a page number, or some other anchoring mark. Then move to the words, sentences, or other portion on which you want the jurors to focus. Zoom right up against the edges of the margins of the text. Eliminate all the white space around the edges of the document. This takes some practice to get to the margins directly without eye-wobbling zooms in and out.

Occasionally, a persuasive point will be enhanced by focusing first on a word or phrase on a page and then zooming out to the full page in order to show that word in context. This technique should be used very sparingly. Jurors have a difficult time focusing on a zoom out and may not be able to follow the point at all.

Highlighting

You can use a yellow highlighter to draw attention to the precise text to which you will be directing the witness's attention. Other colors are available if you need to make related or contrasting points, but yellow is generally most effective for highlighting. Most often, you will want to pre-mark the exhibit with the highlighting you intend to use. Occasionally you may want to mark the text yourself as the witness proceeds. This technique should be reserved for unusual occasions where this method of emphasis is needed because you are responding to an unexpected point. The action of highlighting distracts the jury's attention from the substance of what is being said.

You can also highlight photos by marking directly on the surface with a colored marker if you have a number of copies of the photo. An easier technique is to put the photo in a plastic sleeve and use a grease pencil to mark on the plastic. This way the sleeve can be marked as a separate exhibit if necessary, and the original photo escapes unscathed. Use a sleeve with a matte finish, not a shiny finish, to avoid glare.

Covers

One way to get the jury to follow text line by line is to put a blank piece of paper on top of the document text and pull it down the page one line at a time.

Sometimes you need to highlight text by blocking out other, irrelevant text. This can be done by laying a blank piece of paper over the portions to be blanked out. This often works better than a prepared exhibit with the irrelevant sections already removed. The jury can see that the material has not really been removed, just covered up to assist their focus. An amazing number of jurors assume that lawyers have done something sneaky when redacted documents appear on the screen. The evidence camera gets around this problem.

Sizing

When you put a small object on the base of the evidence camera, put a normal ruler next to the object. As you zoom to enlarge the object, the tick marks on the ruler will also enlarge and keep the size of the object in perspective.

Pointing

A pencil or pen tip works well as a pointer to direct attention to features of the object being displayed on the evidence camera. Special purpose pointers are also available. In some instances, you can simply point with your finger. One problem with this approach is that your viewers may concentrate on your fingernails rather than the exhibit. It is difficult to use your finger as a pointer for a small object because the enlarged image of the fingertip may obliterate the view of the object.

Background

A white object on the base does not produce a good image on the screen. Use a piece of colored construction paper on the base and set the white object on top of it to create the necessary contrast. Blue or green paper is usually a good background. Light colors, and particularly yellow, do not work well as a background because they mislead the iris on the camera. The auto-iris decreases the amount of light to compensate for the light background and the image gets darker. Darker colors like dark brown or black also may cause problems because they absorb light. Before trial, try out the color scheme you intend to use to ensure that the resulting image is clear and sharp.

Exhibits in color

The color switch on the evidence camera activates an automatic enhancement for color images. In rare cases, you might want to display an exhibit that contains color as a black and white image. To do this, use the black & white switch. For example, color photos of injuries are deemed too gory (and therefore unduly prejudicial) to display to a jury. If an objection of this kind is successful, one option is to display the photo in black and white.

Order of presentation

If you are presenting an object, it is useful for the jury to see the object in "real-life size" first, perhaps accompanied by an introductory explanation from the witness before the object is put on the evidence camera base. If the "real thing" is totally unfamiliar to the average juror and it is important to the case, use a large board with a blowup of a photo or a diagram before introducing the "real thing." After these initial steps, go to the evidence camera for the explanation of the details.

For example, if the issue is the failure of a small unremarkable switch that is part of a large piece of machinery, the lawyer might want to start out with a large diagram or photo mounted on a board illustrating the major features of the machine and the location of the switch and its connections. After the witness explains this overview, the machine can be brought in and identified so the switch can be pointed out. Then, for a detailed explanation of the elements making up the switch, this very small part can be put under the evidence camera so an enlarged view appears on the screen. As the expert explains, the evidence camera operator (or the expert herself) can rotate the

Easy Tech: Cases and Materials on Courtroom Technology
© The National Institute for Trial Advocacy

switch on its side to look at if from that angle, turn it over to look at the underside, and flick it on and off. The jury watches the action and, with this orientation, even the least technically proficient juror will feel comfortable with the presentation. This "live action" capability to display an object makes the evidence camera a better choice than a static blowup of a photo taken from one angle or even a series of photos taken from different angles.

Orientation in opening statement

The opening statement must introduce the technology and the operator, if you are using one, even if the judge has described the equipment generally in her opening instructions. The opening should point out each item of equipment and tell the jury briefly how it is used. Reassure jurors that they will have hard copy of every exhibit when they go to the jury room, and tell them that the equipment is primarily for the purpose of saving time.

The more technology you plan to use in the trial, the more you will need to keep the beginning of the opening statement low tech and personal. Jurors will only accept what you present on a screen or monitor if they accept you as the person who is delivering the display. An evidence camera is very low tech and can be made quite personal if the lawyer delivering the opening operates the equipment directly. It is particularly effective against an opponent who uses PowerPoint slides a great deal. The evidence camera shows the "real thing" (an enlargement of a photo, a good view of a small object, a portion of text from a document) and contrasts well against bullet point summaries.

Relation to the witness

The evidence camera is a supporting prop, not the star of the show. Except for witnesses called only to authenticate exhibits, it should make very limited appearance until the witness has firmly established credibility through presentation of material that allows the jury to assess the witness as a person and as a credible actor in the context of the trial. This is particularly important where the strategy is to call the expert first to explain the theory of the case. If the jury does not buy the expert as a person, they will reject the expert's theory.

Individual witnesses relate to an evidence camera differently. Some are most effective if they concentrate on testifying, while the lawyer controls the display and points to the items the witness is explaining. Others are at their best when they come down off the stand, walk to the evidence camera, and put on their own displays pointing to significant items so that the pointer appears with the image on the screen. The witness as an operator is a very effective way to present evidence, and some courtrooms are equipped with evidence cameras at the witness stand for this purpose. When the person with the information (not the lawyer advocate) is at the controls of the information being delivered, jurors may be significantly more receptive and interested. However, controlling the display while talking in the high-stress environment of a courtroom is more than some witnesses can handle.

Objections

The normal way to deal with objections is to remove the exhibit from under the exhibit camera as soon as an objection is made. After the court rules, if the objection is overruled, the exhibit can be put back under the exhibit camera as the examination of the witness proceeds.

Easy Tech: Cases and Materials on Courtroom Technology
© The National Institute for Trial Advocacy

PROBLEMS

1. Take an object out of your pocket or bag, put it on the evidence camera, and in ninety seconds or less, do the following (as if the object were an exhibit in a case in which you were representing a party):

    *   Identify it as Exhibit 1 and state to the jury what it is.
    *   Zoom in enough so that the viewer can see what the object is and explain briefly.
    *   Zoom in further on a detail (a number, logo, insignia, label) and, when the camera is correctly focused on the detail, explain what it is.
    *   Turn the object over or around to reveal a second detail. Focus the camera as necessary. Explain what that detail is.
    *   Zoom out to leave the evidence camera in the proper focus for the next exhibit.

2. Using the photo that is Exhibit 2 in this chapter (or any other suitable photo):

    *   Identify it as Exhibit 2 and state to the jury what it is.
    *   Zoom in enough so that the whole photo fills the screen, and describe the photo.
    *   Zoom in further on a specific detail, and describe it.
    *   Zoom out to leave the evidence camera in the proper focus for the next exhibit.

3. Using the newspaper column that is Exhibit 3 in this chapter:

    *   Identify it as Exhibit 3 and state to the jury what it is.
    *   Zoom in on the dateline, and explain that this reports a decision in a case in California.
    *   Zoom in on a paragraph.
    *   Use a yellow marker or a pen to highlight specific words as you explain what it is.
    *   Zoom out to leave the evidence camera in the proper focus for the next exhibit.

Easy Tech: Cases and Materials on Courtroom Technology
© The National Institute for Trial Advocacy

EXHIBIT 2

The Garden of Earthly Delights
Hieronymous Bosch
c. 1510

EXHIBIT 3

Court Ruling Boosts Photographers Rights On Web and Beyond

By a Wall Street Journal *Staff Reporter*

SAN FRANCISCO – In a ruling that strengthens the rights of photographers on the Internet and beyond, the Ninth U.S. Circuit Court of Appeals this week decided that digitally altered photographs are protected by copyright laws.

The ruling, which overturns a previous decision by the U.S. District Court of Northern California, was heralded as a watershed by photographers. Digital-alteration software and the widespread distribution on the Web have thwarted the efforts of many photographers to enforce copyright protections of their pictures.

"This decision is another safety net on that slippery slope that we seem to be on, where copyright rights are continually challenged and threatened." said Victor Perlman, general counsel of American Society of Media Photographers in Philadelphia.

The dispute revolved around a photograph of the 1991 America's Cup yacht race taken by Jeffrey Hunter Mendler. **Winterland Concessions** Co., a clothing manufacturer based in San Leandro, Calif., licensed the photographs for use on T-shirts in 1992, but then digitally altered them for use again in 1995.

Mr. Mendler sued Winterland for copyright infringement. Winterland argued that the alterations–which included changing the color scheme from blues to browns to gray and violet, flipping and elongating the picture and adding text and graphics–amounted to creating a new image.

The lower court supported Winterland, saying that the licensing agreement allowed Winterland to tamper with the photograph. But in a 2-1 decision, the appeals court agreed with Mr. Mendler.

2.   THE LAPTOP COMPUTER, PRESENTATION SOFTWARE, AND PROJECTOR

Computer-based technology in the courtroom draws from the same strength as older methods like the blackboard, the flip chart, and the overhead projector. Getting points across visually is far more powerful and persuasive than relying solely on oral means. Not only is this a more audience-friendly way to project key facts, images and arguments in a case, but science has verified that this information sticks longer and more clearly in the minds of jurors.

The most basic courtroom setup includes a laptop computer, entry level presentation software, a lightweight digital projector, and a eight-foot or ten-foot projection screen. The computer is plugged into an electrical outlet and connected via a cable to the projector, the projection screen is set up in a location where everyone can see it, and the projector is positioned sixteen to twenty feet away from and directly in front of the projection screen. The objective is to get evidentiary exhibits and illustrative aids onto the screen efficiently without dimming the lights in the courtroom.

This equipment can be set up quickly and taken down when not needed. The laptop computer, projector, and cable can be put in a single small carrying case. A newer model screen will fold up into a relatively small package. The entire kit weighs about twenty-five pounds. The cost of purchase or rental is within reach for most lawyers.

This book focuses on the basic level of evidence presentation technology. Alternatives abound. Instead of entry level presentation software designed for many business and sales uses, you can substitute special-purpose (and considerably more expensive) trial presentation software. Instead of a projector and screen, you may be in a courtroom already equipped with monitors so all you have to do is plug in your computer and light up the courtroom. Similarly, you may want to rent large flat panel or conventional monitors instead of using a projector and screen. These alternatives may allow some additional flexibility, but all involve the same underlying techniques explained here.

A.   Best uses

The laptop computer with presentation software is usually the best method for presenting material that needs to build a display, component by component, so that as you explain the jury sees things one point or one part at a time. The computer builds graphics display, plays video excerpts, adds highlights and labels, and keeps track of a large number of exhibits.

Bullet point lists

Bulleted lists work well when driven by a computer because they can be revealed one at a time as the lawyer speaks. That way, the jury is not reading ahead. The computer screen can accommodate only five or six one-line points. This imposes a useful limitation on design. Bulleted lists are the easiest materials to present using a laptop computer because, once the slide show is loaded, the lawyer need only tap the space bar to move from one point to the next. Learning the timing is easy.

Advantages of Bullet Lists

1. Revealed one at a time

2. Jury not reading ahead

3. Encourages pithy statements

4. Control by click or tap

5. Timing easy to learn

Easy Tech: Cases and Materials on Courtroom Technology
© The National Institute for Trial Advocacy

Text documents

The computer is usually the best alternative for working with text documents in a courtroom. Computer graphics such as boxes or circles around key words, callouts emphasizing important text, and even simple enlargements of cropped portions of text allow the lawyer to keep the jury's focus on the point at hand. The ability to reveal one item at a time is important in progressing smoothly and persuasively through an explanation or an examination about a text document.

Charts and graphs

Statistical charts, organization charts, relationship charts, diagrams, and maps do well on a computer-driven display. Charts benefit from the ability to reveal one item at a time, and maps and diagrams often need labels, arrows, and explanations that are best provided with computer graphics.

Time Lines

If the passage of time, in either minutes, days, or years, or the juxtaposition of events is significant, then a time line can be very effective to explain the meaning given by the time reference. When the state of the art in graphics was the use of "big boards," time lines were often too long, too large, the print too small, and the data points too many. The more flexible technique of computer-generated graphics allows for time lines that build entry by entry. This enables the lawyer to focus the jury on the single entry that best serves a particular point. Additional data points and expanded explanations can be added as an opening statement or witness testimony moves on.

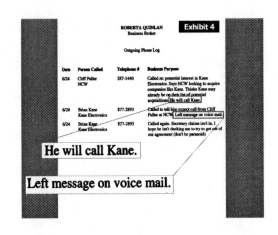

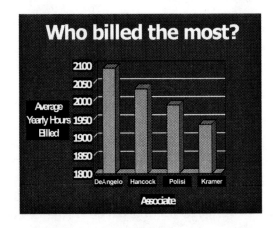

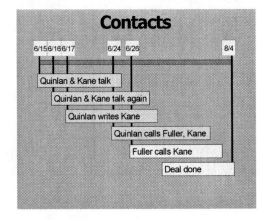

Easy Tech: Cases and Materials on Courtroom Technology
© The National Institute for Trial Advocacy

Scientific, Medical or Technical Graphics

In most cases, the jury must learn at least some scientific, medical or technical information in order to decide the case. Often these areas are complex and the subject of extensive expert testimony. It may be useful to introduce these concepts early, even in opening statement, to teach the jury enough of the science to allow them to understand the testimony as it is presented. This will have the added benefit of enhancing the lawyer's credibility as one who understands and can demonstrate the relevant principles. Exhibits from the case, such as CT scans, diagrams, and technical drawings can be incorporated and displayed through the same

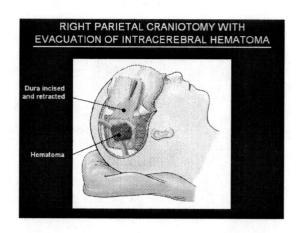

presentation software. Beyond simply displaying technical graphics, these exhibits can be labeled, highlighted or annotated to underscore their significance.

Video clips

Video taped deposition snippets provide excellent opportunities for high impact use in opening statement and for impeachment. All of this can be easily and dramatically portrayed through the computer. A typical display includes the video and soundtrack. Alternatively, the video can be displayed at the top of the screen with the transcript scrolling below as the witness speaks. The video can be stopped and started again during cross-examination or to emphasize particularly important parts of the testimony during closing argument.

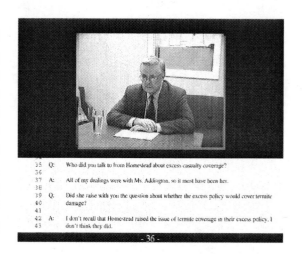

B.   Operation

There are two principal software packages: PowerPoint for users of the Microsoft office suite of applications programs, and Corel Presentations for users of the WordPerfect office suite of similar programs. You can use either one.

Entry level presentation software uses the slide show metaphor—individual visual displays are "slides": and groups of related visuals are "slide shows." The operation of a laptop computer and projector setup involves opening the slide show where the exhibits and illustrative aids are stored, starting the show, and using the computer keyboard to move forward or backward within the slide show. The mouse has comparable controls, and special remote controls are available for most projectors as alternatives to using the laptop's keyboard.

Easy Tech: Cases and Materials on Courtroom Technology
© The National Institute for Trial Advocacy

Using PowerPoint, the basic operations are as follows.

To open the slide show: Turn on the computer, click on the START button at the bottom left corner of the screen, click on the Programs option on the first menu, then click on the PowerPoint option on the second menu. With the PowerPoint software opened, click on the option on the initial dialog box labeled "Open an existing presentation." The case files are on the CD that accompanies this book. With the CD in the CD drive on the laptop, go to the CD drive, and open the file.

To start the slide show: Go to the View Bar at the lower left corner of the screen which has five buttons. Click on the Slide Show button which is the last one on the right.

To move from one slide to the next within the show: Press the SPACEBAR on the keyboard once to move forward to the next slide. Press the BACKSPACE KEY on the keyboard once to move back to the previous slide.

To stop the slide show: Press the ESC key on the keyboard.

For more information, consult *PowerPoint for Litigators* (NITA 2000).

Using Corel Presentations, the basic operations are as follows.

To open the slide show: Turn on the computer, click on the START button at the bottom left corner of the screen, click on the Programs option on the first menu, then click on the Corel Presentations (or WordPerfect Office suite) option on the second menu. With the Corel Presentations software opened, go to the Menu Bar, click on the File button, and select the Open option on the menu. The case files are on the CD that accompanies this book. With the CD in the CD drive on the laptop, go to the CD drive, and open the file.

To start the slide show: Go to the tabs at the far right side of the screen. Click on the QuickPlay tab which is the last one toward the bottom.

To move from one side to the next within the show: Press the SPACEBAR on the keyboard once to move forward to the next slide. Press the BACKSPACE KEY on the keyboard once to move back to the previous slide.

To stop the slide show: Press the ESC key on the keyboard.

For more information, consult *Corel Presentations for Litigators* (NITA, 2000).

      C.   Setup

The courtroom setup for a laptop and projector is the same as shown in Section 1(C) with respect to the evidence camera. The laptop is at the lawyer's podium or table and is cabled directly to the digital projector. The projector and screen are set up so that the jury has an unobstructed view of the screen. If possible, the screen should be located straight across from the jury box. You need about twice the distance from the first row of seats as the size of the screen. A six-foot screen will be twelve feet from the audience; and eight-foot screen will be sixteen feet away; and a ten-foot screen will be twenty feet away.

Cabling

The laptop computer is cabled directly to the digital projector using computer cabling. The setup needs only two connections, one at either end of the cable.

Most laptop computers have a toggle switch that controls the screen display by permitting three alternatives: display only on the computer's screen, display only on the projector's screen, or display on both screens at once. Each manufacturer places these controls somewhat differently, but they are usually operated by a combination of keys. One of the keys will usually have a small icon representing a large screen together with a computer screen. Be sure that the computer setting is for both screens at once. Toggle through the alternatives until you get to this one.

D.   Techniques in using the laptop and projector

A very large projection screen displaying compelling images competes effectively for the attention of the jury. If they are watching the screen, they are not watching you. If they are not watching you, it may be that they are not listening to you either. Therefore, when you use a large screen, you need to be mindful of this competition for the jury's attention and use the screen in a way that complements your presentation. The principal techniques for making the evidence presentation more effective using a laptop computer to drive visual displays are set out below.

Focus on the audience

When a trial lawyer speaks, it should be to the judge or the jury. A lawyer should not wind up speaking to or reading material from the screen. The temptation to look at the screen is strong because you want to see if it really is displaying what you expect. Absent some extraordinary malfunction, if the image is on your computer's screen, and if the projector was tested and found to be operating properly before you began your presentation, the image will also be on the big screen.

Position in relation to the screen

Stand somewhere in front of the screen where you are not blocking the audience's view of the screen. Look directly at the audience in the same way that you would if you had no visuals on the screen behind you. The visuals reinforce your oral presentation; they do not replace it.

Timing and pauses

Give attention to the order in which you plan to make the oral point and the visual point. Sometimes it is useful to display the visual before you start the oral explanation. For example, the trial lawyer displays the enlarged and labeled photo of the office building on Main Street, pauses while the audience looks at the photo, and then says: "This is the office building that burned down on the night of January 12." More often, you will find that the timing works better if you make the oral point, show the visual, pause while the visual is absorbed, and then explain the point. In an opening statement, when using bullet point lists to help set the chronology, the trial lawyer might state the first point, then display the first point on the screen, then go on to explain it.

Easy Tech: Cases and Materials on Courtroom Technology
© The National Institute for Trial Advocacy

Pauses are important in making presentations using significant visuals. Your audience will be impatient with you if you rush along, not giving them a chance to absorb what is on the screen. The silence may seem long to you, but it is comfortable for them.

Black slides

A slide that is colored entirely black will cause the screen to go blank. There are always times during any presentation that you want the focus to be entirely on you. To make the screen's competition disappear, you can just turn off the image by using a black slide. These slides can be placed strategically throughout the slide show. You can also tap the B key on your computer keyboard if you are using PowerPoint. That will turn off the image and keep the screen dark until you tap the B key again to turn it on.

Black slides are important at the beginning and at the end of any slide show. A black slide at the beginning of the slide show allows you to set up the computer and projector and keep all the equipment on until you are ready to use it, but without anything on the screen. A black slide at the end of the slide show is a crisp way to end. If you leave the last slide on the screen, it may not match the ending you plan to make. If you go beyond the last slide, with no black slide in place, you will display the thumbnails of all your slides for the audience to see. The black slide is a fail-safe mechanism.

Light hand on the controls

A trial lawyer's angst at using presentation technology is often expressed most clearly in the mannerisms accompanying the use of the controls. Whether you are tapping the SPACEBAR, clicking the left mouse button, or pressing a button on a hand-held remote, you need to appear to be at ease with the task. Twitching, clutching, and nervous glances at the equipment expecting imminent failure makes your audience aware that you are uncomfortable with the equipment. They expect the kind of seamless ease that they see on television, and they are distracted by anything less.

Backup

Any laptop presentation should include backup plans in the event that the equipment fails. One way to deal with backup is to have available a second laptop loaded with all the same files. Another method is to have printouts of the thumbnails of the slides that you plan to present. If the computer fails, you can use the evidence camera to display the thumbnails suitably enlarged.

Objections

The normal way to deal with objections is to remove the exhibit from the screen as soon as an objection is made. If the court or bailiff has a kill switch, normally that is the mechanism used to remove the slide from the screen while the objection is heard. If there is no kill switch, the lawyer has three alternatives: (1) PowerPoint users can press the B key (for black screen) on the keyboard and the screen will go black; pressing the B key again will bring back the exhibit. (2) Note the slide number where you are, and press the CTRL key plus the number that corresponds to the slide number of a black slide, which will bring the black slide to the screen. Pressing CTRL and the number of the slide where you were when the objection arose will bring the contested slide back. (3) Use the toggle switch (explained in subsection C above) to turn off the external monitors.

Easy Tech: Cases and Materials on Courtroom Technology
© The National Institute for Trial Advocacy

PROBLEMS

1.   Seven bullet point slides are on the CD that comes with this book. They are in a folder labeled Part 1, and they are stored as separate slide shows. They should be downloaded from the CD to the hard disk drive of the laptop computer used for this exercise. Using your presentation software, open all the slide shows. When you go to the Menu Bar at the top of the screen and click on the Windows button, all seven are listed. They also appear as Exhibits 3, 4, 5, 6, 7, 8 and 9 in this chapter. Each bullet point slide has four to six separate points. These points will appear one at a time as you press the space bar.

- Pick one of the slides.
- Do a one-minute presentation using each of the points on the slide. You can either recite the familiar material, or do a mock opening statement or closing argument in the mythical cases that arose from these circumstances.
- The title of the slide will appear first. Press the space bar on the computer keyboard when you want to advance from one point to the next on the slide.

2.   Ten bullet point slides—Exhibits 10, 11, 12, 13, 14, 15, 16, 17, 18, 19 and 20—are on the CD. As each is displayed, critique its design and appropriateness as an illustrative aid used for the direct case. You may want to comment on:

- Choice of words
- Length of points
- Typeface and type size
- Color
- Transition (which brings the slide to the screen)
- Animation (of individual objects on the slide)
- Other factors in the design of the slide

Night Before Christmas

'Twas the night before Christmas
And all through the house
Not a creature was stirring
Not even a mouse
The stockings were hung
By the chimney with care
In hopes that St. Nicholas
Soon would be there

```
┌─────────────────────────────┐
│      December 24th          │
└─────────────────────────────┘

  • Christmas eve
  • House quiet
  • Fireplace ready
  • Awaiting Santa
```

Jack and Jill

Jack and Jill
Went up the hill
To fetch a pail of water
Jack fell down
And broke his crown
And Jill came tumbling after

```
┌─────────────────────────────┐
│    Jack and Jill's Accident │
└─────────────────────────────┘

  • Jack and Jill climb hill
  • Jack falls
  • Fractures skull
  • Jill falls, too
```

Three Blind Mice

Three blind mice
See how they run
They all ran after the farmer's wife
She cut off their tails with a carving knife
Did you ever see such a sight in your life
As three blind mice

```
┌─────────────────────────────┐
│      Three Abused Mice      │
└─────────────────────────────┘

  • Three visually challenged mice
  • Still great runners
  • Chased farmer's wife
  • Caught and tortured by farmer
  • Maimed for life
```

Easy Tech: Cases and Materials on Courtroom Technology
© The National Institute for Trial Advocacy

Little Jack Horner

Little Jack Horner
Sat in a corner
Eating his Christmas pie
He stuck in his thumb
And pulled out a plum
And said, "What a good boy am I"

Mary Had a Little Lamb

Mary had a little lamb
Its fleece was white as snow
And everywhere that Mary went
The lamb was sure to go
It followed her to school one day
Which was against the rule
It made the children laugh and play
To see a lamb at school

Old Mother Hubbard

Old Mother Hubbard
Went to the cupboard
To fetch her poor dog a bone
But when she got there
The cupboard was bare
And so the poor dog had none

Twinkle, Twinkle, Little Star

Twinkle, twinkle, little star
How I wonder what you are
Up above the world so high
Like a diamond in the sky
Twinkle, twinkle, little star
How I wonder what you are

Easy Tech: Cases and Materials on Courtroom Technology
© The National Institute for Trial Advocacy

3.   THE TELESTRATOR

The telestrator is a hardware device that works with the evidence camera and with a laptop to allow the user to mark the image on the screen in various ways. This device provides the capability for the lawyer or witness to put pointers on the screen, to draw directional arrows, circles, shading, or even to label objects. It is also known as a "John Madden pen" after the sports commentator who made the technique widely popular (although Madden actually uses a light pen, not a telestrator), and as the "illustrator" (although it is not very good at creating illustrations of anything).

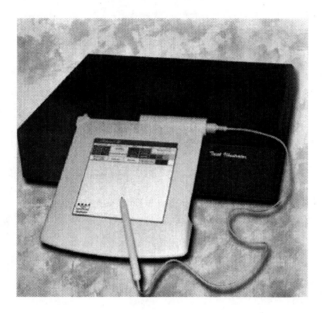

The telestrator enhances the control that the lawyer or witness has in explaining the image on the screen. If a part of a photo might be difficult for the audience to find from a verbal description (e.g., the northwest corner of the second intersection), the telestrator allows the lawyer or witness to draw an arrow or create a pointer (e.g., this point on the photo that I have marked, which is the northwest corner . . .). When the explanation has been completed, the marks can be erased instantly with a tap of the pen leaving the exhibit unchanged.

The telestrator works well with an evidence camera or a laptop setup because the pen is used on a tablet and not on the surface of a computer monitor. The evidence camera typically has no associated monitor, and a laptop has a soft screen that cannot tolerate any kind of pen marks. An equivalent unit, the light pen, is sometimes used at the witness stand. Its pen is used directly on the hard glass surface of a standard external computer monitor. The marks and controls are about the same. Presentation software also offers on-screen drawing capability through mouse controls.

The telestrator tablet is about nine inches square. It has no special mounting requirements. The unit will sit on any table or other level surface. Its supporting hardware box is about the size of a laptop, and connects to a standard electrical outlet through a power strip to guard against unusual spikes in the electrical current.

Easy Tech: Cases and Materials on Courtroom Technology
© The National Institute for Trial Advocacy

A. Best uses

The telestrator is most effective when it is used to make simple, definitive marks on the image that are for the purpose of making introductory or subordinate points. The marks made by the telestrator usually will be erased as the presentation proceeds. They will not appear on the exhibit and are usually not preserved in the record. The use of the telestrator is similar to the lawyer pointing to something on a hard copy enlargement that has been propped up on an easel. When you are using a projector and screen, it is better to put electronically generated marks on the screen than to use the traditional methods. If you point to something on the screen, you will usually get between the projector and the screen and a portion of the screen will be occupied by the shadow of your arm or hand. This is distracting to the viewer. The telestrator overcomes this problem.

If you want the witness to make the marks on the image that has been projected on the screen, and there is a light pen at the witness stand, the witness can use that equipment in the same way as described below. If there is no equipment at the witness stand, the witness can step down to the telestrator and make the marks in the same way as a witness might step down to an exhibit to point out specific features.

Markers or pointers

The telestrator has twelve types of markers or pointers that can be placed on the image. The controls are quite flexible. These shapes can be used in any one of seven colors that appear on the color pad on the tablet. The pointer is placed on the image with a tap of the pen. Several pointers can be used on the same image. They can be removed one by one or all pointers can be cleared at the same time.

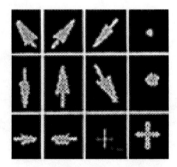

Lines, arrows, or circles

The telestrator's pen can be used to draw simple line or arrow shapes to point out a particular feature of the exhibit. The tablet has controls to vary the width of the line and the seven colors on the color pad can be used for individual lines or arrows. Like pointers, lines and arrows can be removed one by one or all can be cleared at the same time.

Simple letters or numbers

Labels such as A, B, or C can be added to an image in order to link the point being made with the witness's testimony to the image at hand. Because the telestrator is sensitive to small variations in motion, it takes a steady hand to create a readable letter. More complicated annotations such as words or illustrations are best done in advance with the presentation software.

Easy Tech: Cases and Materials on Courtroom Technology

B.   Operation

The operation of the telestrator involves simply placing the pen on the drawing space on the tablet, pressing gently, and moving the pen to make the desired marks. To anchor yourself visually, look at the image on the screen, not the tablet. Make a small initial mark to see where your pen is in relation to the image on the screen. Then move the pen and make the necessary marks, keeping your eye on the screen. Normal eye-hand coordination will get the pen to the right place.

The telestrator has five components.

1.   Hardware box

The electronics that produce the marks on the screen are contained in a box about the size of a laptop computer.

2.   Tablet pad

The tablet contains the surface on which the user makes the marks that are replicated on top of the image on the screen. It also contains the switches for the various pointer shapes and line widths and colors available with the system.

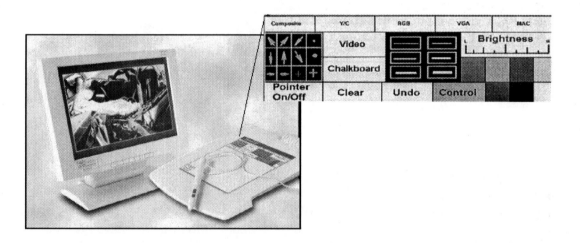

3.   Pen

The pen is the control for the unit. By moving its point across the tablet, the user creates the marks to be put on the image that is being projected by the evidence camera or the laptop. The hardware converts the position and movements of the pen into marks on the screen.

4.   Converter

The telestrator is an analog device. Its output cannot be used directly by digital projectors. The analog signal must be converted to digital format by a converter.

Newer portable projectors have an on-board converter to accommodate the telestrator. With older projectors, you will need a converter called a line doubler between the telestrator and the projector. The line doubler processes the signal coming from the telestrator so that the projector can utilize it.

5.   Cables

The pen is cabled to the tablet. The tablet is cabled to the hardware box. The hardware box is cabled between the output unit (either the evidence camera or the laptop) on one side and the display (either monitors or a projector) on the other side.

The controls are simple and straightforward. They are located on the top section of the tablet and they look like this.

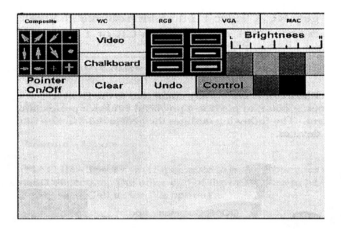

Image on/off

The boxes marked Video and Chalkboard turn the image from the evidence camera or laptop on and off. Tap Video to turn the image on. Tap Chalkboard to turn the image off. When the image is turned off, the display screen is blue. The off switch is called "Chalkboard" because this option allows the user to write words or phrases in the same manner as a blackboard might be used. This technique is sometimes used for business and commercial purposes, but it is generally not used for litigation because handwriting on a large screen is too shaky. The words are full of unintended squiggles. This is distracting in a courtroom.

Pointers on/off

The unit produces either a pointer shape or a line. When the pointer is on, the line is off. To switch between these two options, use the Pointer On/Off box in the lower left corner of the control panel. Tap the box with the pen, and the unit will switch from one mode to the other.

Easy Tech: Cases and Materials on Courtroom Technology
© The National Institute for Trial Advocacy

Pointer shape

When you turn the pointer on, you can choose among twelve pointer shapes. The pointer shapes are in the box at the upper left of the control pad. Tap the desired shape with the pen. When you use the pen to put a pointer on the screen, this shape will be used until you change it. You can change the pointer shape as many times as necessary.

Stationary pointer on/off

The pointer may be used in a mobile mode, when it moves wherever the pen moves, or in a stationary mode, when it is inserted onto an image and stays put. To make the pointer remain in one place, place the tip of the pen at the place where you want the pointer and press the button on the side of the pen.

Line width

When you turn the pointer off, the pen will produce a line when moved across the tablet. The line width controls in the center of the control pad allow you to vary the width of the line. Tap the desired width with the pen. The line width will remain set until you tap a different width.

Color

The telestrator has seven colors which can be applied either to pointers or to lines. The color palette is at the right side of the control pad. Tap the box of the desired color. That color will remain set until you tap a different color.

Brightness

The brightness scale is at the upper right corner of the control pad. The left side of the scale is the darkest and the right side of the scale is the brightest. Choose the degree of brightness by tapping the pen at a point on the scale.

Erase

The Clear and Undo boxes at the bottom center of the control pad take marks off the screen. Undo takes the last mark off the screen. Clear takes all marks off the screen at once. The two erase functions affect only the marks made on the image. The underlying image is not affected.

Control on/off

The telestrator hardware box will support two tablets. For instance, one tablet could be at the witness stand and another tablet at the lawyer's podium. When the lawyer wants to mark on the image, the lawyer's tablet must take "control" of the telestrator unit. The lawyer taps the control box to do this. When the witness wants to mark on the image, the witness's tablet must take "control." The witness taps on the control box on the tablet at the witness stand in order to do this.

Easy Tech: Cases and Materials on Courtroom Technology
© The National Institute for Trial Advocacy

<u>Input sources</u>

The input from an evidence camera going to a digital projector or from a laptop going to a digital projector, which are the two principal litigation uses, uses the "composite" setting at the top left corner of the control panel.

The telestrator unit is designed to be used in commercial and sales presentations. For this reason, it accommodates the three main types of video input: VGA, S-video (Y/C), and NTSC (RCA). Switches for these various inputs are at the top of the control pad. In order to use these settings, the video signal from the input device has to be the same as the video signal that is accepted by the output device. (If the telestrator receives a VGA signal from the input, it can only output a VGA signal to the display.) If the display device (projector or monitor) requires a different type of signal, then a converter is needed. The telestrator is also designed to be used with Macintosh computers. The MAC in and MAC out connections are for this purpose.

C.   Setup

The telestrator fits into the setup for the evidence camera (Section 1(C)) or the laptop computer (Section 2(C)). It does not affect the placement of these input devices or the output devices (projector and screen) in the courtroom.

The telestrator is an in-line overlay device. That means it is placed "in line" between the input device and the output device, and it overlays its marks (pointers, lines, circles, arrows, letters) on the image going from the input device to the output device. For this reason, it has two types of cabling: cabling between the parts of the telestrator (hardware unit, tablet, and pen); and cabling between the telestrator unit and the input (evidence camera or laptop) and output (projector or monitor) equipment.

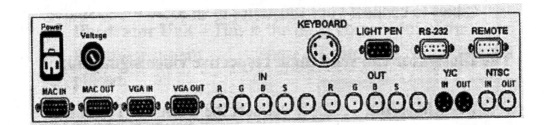

The cabling for the parts of the telestrator unit is straightforward.

- Power: The power cable connects the telestrator to the electrical outlet in the courtroom.

- Voltage: The voltage selector switch should always be set at 110 volts.

Easy Tech: Cases and Materials on Courtroom Technology
© The National Institute for Trial Advocacy

- Tablet: The cable from the tablet is connected to the keyboard connection and to the RS-232 connection.

- Pen: The cable from the pen to the tablet is permanently affixed.

The cabling between the telestrator and the input and output devices requires care but is easy to accomplish. If the input is from an evidence camera, the input cable coming from the evidence camera is connected to the NTSC IN jack. The output to the projector is connected from the NTSC OUT jack.

If the input is from a laptop, the input cable coming from the laptop is connected to the VGA IN jack. The output to the projector is connected from the VGA OUT jack.

If your courtroom setup includes both an evidence camera and a laptop as potential input sources, you will need a switch device in line from the two inputs that allows you to switch from one input to another.

Once cabled properly, there is relatively little that can go wrong with the telestrator.

Blue screen on display

If the input device (evidence camera or laptop) is operating, the telestrator unit is operating, and the screen display is blue (rather than projecting the image that has been selected), check to see if the Chalkboard option is active. Press the Video option on the control pad to restore the image.

White screen on display

If the input device is operating, the telestrator unit is operating, and the screen display is white (rather than projecting the image that has been selected), the signal is not reaching the projector. Check the cabling between the input device and the telestrator and between the telestrator and the projector. Check the setting on the projector, which may need to be adjusted to accommodate the telestrator.

D. Techniques in using the telestrator

Steady hand

The telestrator pen will transmit to the screen any motion it receives. If your hand is unsteady, the line on the screen will have wiggles in it. To prevent this, grasp the pen in a comfortable position, but gently. Move the pen in relatively swift, decisive strokes.

Gentle pressure

The tip of the telestrator pen is designed both to choose options from the control pad and to transmit motion to the tablet. It requires only a gentle press on the tip to select an option from the control pad. Pressing harder may confuse the unit into duplicating your command several times.

Easy Tech: Cases and Materials on Courtroom Technology
© The National Institute for Trial Advocacy

<u>Simple annotations</u>

The telestrator works best in a litigation setting when it is used for relatively simple annotations. An arrow to point out the particular aspect of the exhibit being discussed by the lawyer or the witness, a circle to highlight a critical number, or pointers at several places to help draw conclusions are all useful annotations. Try to avoid writing words, drawing shapes more complicated than a circle or an arrow, or using long numbers.

E.   Software alternatives: the annotation pen

Entry level presentation software provides an annotation pen feature that offers a more limited drawing capability. The pen feature turns the mouse pointer into a pen so that when you hold down the left mouse button and move the mouse, a line drawing appears on the screen. The width and color of the line can be changed with alternatives similar to the telestrator. This software works only with input from a laptop. To get drawing capability for an image generated by an evidence camera, the hardware capability of the telestrator is necessary.

The two principal entry level presentation software packages are Microsoft's PowerPoint and Corel's Presentations. Each has a pen feature readily accessible.

In PowerPoint: Press CTRL + P to change the mouse pointer into a draw capability. The mouse pointer shape will change to a pen. Hold down the left mouse button and move the mouse on the screen. The mouse pointer will draw lines. Let up on the left mouse button at the end of the line. Press the E key on the keyboard to erase the mouse drawings from the screen while still keeping the pen feature active. Press CTRL + A to move the mouse pointer back to its normal arrow shape. The next mouse click will remove the mouse drawings from the screen. To change the pen color before the show, go the Menu Bar, click on the Slide Show option, then click on the Set Up Show option, then go to the Pen Color box in the lower left corner of the dialog box and set the color. To change the color during the show, right click with the mouse, click on the Pointer Options choice, then click on the Pen Color option.

In Corel Presentations: When you are in Slide Show mode (the QuickPlay tab has been activated), the mouse has a draw capability. Hold down the left mouse button. The mouse pointer shape turns to a crayon. When you move the mouse around the screen (while still holding down the left mouse button), it will draw lines. Click once to take the drawings off the screen while keeping the slide on the screen. To change the color of the pen feature, go to the Menu Bar, click on the View button, then click on the Play Slide Show option. The Play Slide Show dialog box will appear. Click on the Highlighter Color button. A color palette will appear. Click on the color you want. The width of the line can also be changed using the Width button at the same location.

The more advanced trial presentation software packages also provide drawing and pointer capabilities. These annotation features have more of the telestrator's capability.

PROBLEMS

1.   There are two photos—Exhibits 21 and 22—on the CD. With the laptop running and one of these photos displayed on the projection screen, use the telestrator or illustrator to:

> Circle an object to identify it, and describe the object as you work.
> Describe how far it is away from another object in the photo, and draw a line from one object to another to point out the distance.
> Change the color of the pen or the width of the line.
> Sign your name.

2.   With the evidence camera running and Exhibit 2 from the evidence camera problems displayed on the projection screen, use the telestrator or illustrator to do the same exercises in problem 1 above.

Easy Tech: Cases and Materials on Courtroom Technology
© The National Institute for Trial Advocacy

PART II: OBJECTIONS

Lawyers face new challenges when the number of visual displays increases substantially and the technology allows them to come and go rapidly. The pace of the entire trial picks up. Careful preparation is at a premium. Most importantly, however, lawyers must now respond quickly and surely to visual cues to objections as well as the oral ones to which they are accustomed. When an examiner asks, "What did Mr. Smith tell you?" the oral cue for hearsay triggers immediate consideration of an objection. When an examiner previews slides for the court, the visual cues to objections are not always instantly apparent. For this reason, knowledgeable lawyers ask the court to require pretrial disclosure of illustrative aids to be used in opening statement or with expert witnesses.

This section describes a practical approach to making and meeting objections when presentation technology is used in a trial. The trial lawyer should first decide whether the thing being displayed is an evidentiary exhibit—that is, something that has been admitted or will be offered in evidence—or an illustrative aid. If it is an evidentiary exhibit, then the objections are, for the most part, not any different than the traditional objections to exhibits. If it is an illustrative aid, some "new" objections may appear. They are discussed below.

1.   EVIDENTIARY EXHIBITS VS. ILLUSTRATIVE AIDS

Each evidentiary exhibit has a foundation that qualifies it as an appropriate basis to be used in deciding the case. This includes the competence of the witness to testify about the exhibit, the relevance of the exhibit to an issue in the case, the identification of the exhibit distinguishing it from all other things; and the trustworthiness or authentication of the exhibit. With respect to documents, this may also include requirements with respect to hearsay and the original documents rule.

Each illustrative aid has a foundation that qualifies it as an appropriate means to assist in the presentation or understanding of the testimony to be given. An illustrative aid was typically prepared for litigation purposes. It has no part in the history of the case, and is not "relevant" under Rule 401. For that reason, it cannot be admitted in evidence. If an evidentiary exhibit (admitted in evidence) has been enhanced in some way, such as with labels, superimposed images, or callouts, it is likely now an illustrative aid. Even if the underlying exhibit has been admitted, the illustrative aid based on that exhibit can be excluded on grounds explained in Section 3, below.

In most courts, evidentiary exhibits may go to the jury room during jury deliberations, but illustrative aids may not. The rationale is that evidentiary exhibits are an appropriate basis for deciding the case, while illustrative aids are not. In order that the jury not confuse the two, most judges simply exclude all illustrative aids.

Evidentiary exhibits and illustrative aids typically are numbered in the same numbering series, without differentiation. For this reason, it is important that a clear record be made as to the category into which each numbered exhibit falls.

Easy Tech: Cases and Materials on Courtroom Technology
© The National Institute for Trial Advocacy

2. OBJECTIONS TO EVIDENTIARY EXHIBITS

When thinking about objections to evidentiary exhibits, it is useful to keep in mind the distinction between evidence shown electronically and evidence that is electronic in nature. This is a distinction between evidence that exists in the first instance in physical form, such as a document or standard photo or physical object, and evidence that exists in the first instance in electronic form, such as photos or video created with digital cameras and digital audio recordings. In addition, the "completeness" objection may have some new variations.

A. Evidence shown electronically

An evidentiary exhibit does not change its character just because it is displayed using courtroom technology. Whether the document is in paper format or an image on a 10-foot projection screen, it is still the same exhibit. Evidence that exists in physical form should present no problem under the original documents rule. Once a sufficient foundation is laid, and the exhibit is admitted in evidence, it can be shown electronically. Any enlargement or display of the exhibit using courtroom technology should require nothing further by way of exhibit numbering or qualification. The display on the projection screen or monitor is the treated the same as the paper copy or physical object that has been admitted.

Lawyers may point out in an objection that the electronic display of the physical evidence is almost always different from the hard copy original because the color and resolution or the original cannot be reproduced with absolute accuracy on the monitor. The differences, however, will be very minor. In the Unabomber trial, the defense sought unsuccessfully to keep the prosecution from displaying the defendant's writings electronically. Because the purpose of the electronic display was an examination of the textual content of the writings, even if the electronic display had to qualify as a duplicate, the slight differences in color and resolution of the images on the screen (as compared to the paper copies) could not meet the test of Rule 1003(2) that "in the circumstances it would be unfair to admit the duplicate in lieu of the original."

B. Evidence that is electronic in nature

Evidence that was created in electronic form and is either converted to physical format for purposes of being admitted in evidence or is displayed electronically for purposes of being admitted in evidence in that format may cause lawyers to raise objections based on the original documents rule. Such objections require the proponent to jump through the hoops of Rules 1001, 1002, and 1003. This is usually done readily.

Under Rule 1002, if the exhibit is a writing or a photograph, then the original is required unless, under Rule 1003, a duplicate may be used instead of the original. The "originals" of writings created with word processing software and photographs or videos created with digital cameras are electronic files. The "duplicates" in most cases are hard copies printed out and marked as exhibits. A duplicate, under Rule 1001(4) is anything produced by a process or technique that accurately reproduces the original. Printing a hard copy is a process that is uniformly accepted in the commercial world as accurately reproducing the original. The courts demand no more. The duplicate is admitted under Rule 1003 unless some unfairness can be demonstrated. The burden in that regard is on the opponent. An alternative is to copy the digital file to a CD. In that case the

Easy Tech: Cases and Materials on Courtroom Technology
© The National Institute for Trial Advocacy

duplicate is the file on the CD. Similarly, the operating system software process that "copies" digital files is uniformly accepted as accurately reproducing the original. Indeed, it is almost never done any other way.

C. Completeness objection

Lawyers are usually referring to Rule 106 when they object to a visual display on the grounds of completeness. That rule covers documents and videotapes of depositions but does not apply to photographs and videotapes of facts relevant to the case. Circumstances may arise under which courts would use the general powers under Rule 611(a) to achieve the same result for materials not covered by Rule 106.

> **Rule 106—Remainder of or Related Writings or Recorded Statements**
>
> When a writing or recorded statement or part thereof is introduced by a party, an adverse party may require the introduction at that time of any other part or any other writing or recorded statement which ought in fairness to be considered contemporaneously with it.

Video

Most videotapes are too long to be shown to a jury with any hope that they will absorb all of the information presented. Excerpts are prepared and information on several videotapes may be combined. If the court requires pretrial disclosure of this kind of exhibit, opposing counsel will be able to consider the editing that has been done to determine if the result is unfair. If the videotape is of a deposition, under Rule 106, the court may consider whether additional portions should be shown.

Counsel may argue about the expense of adding portions to their prepared video clips. Expense is normally not a significant factor. If the video was shot with a digital camera, adding portions is akin to copying and adding paragraphs in word processing and can be done very quickly. If the video was shot with a regular camera, digitizing (changing it from analog to digital format) is an automated process done by many suppliers. However, timing can be a problem. It is not always possible to get this done overnight. For this reason, most knowledgeable lawyers digitize much more of the videotape than they plan to use, or shoot the entire videotape with a digital camera.

Still frames extracted from video may also present a problem. Digital technology makes it much easier to pick one frame from hours of video and to enlarge and use that frame as a still photo. Because video involves so many frames, normally seen in context, taking one frame out of context may be unfair. A disclosure rule will allow counsel to know from what video the still photo came and to decide if it is potentially unfair because it has been taken out of context.

Photos

Any photo taken with a digital camera is in the form of a digital file. Any photo taken with a regular camera can be turned into a digital file. That is done by putting it on a scanner, closing the lid, and pressing the button to make a scan (or an "image"), which is a process not unlike photocopying as far as time, expense, and operator skill are concerned.

Easy Tech: Cases and Materials on Courtroom Technology
© The National Institute for Trial Advocacy

Cropping is a process in which parts of the photo are cut away. For example, the photo of the Orlando courtroom shown below can be cropped to show just one desk with one monitor on it, or to show a portion of the courtroom in which there are no monitors at all, as shown below.

There is nothing inherently unfair about cropping, but cropping can also be used to create images that are, in fact, unfair given the context in which they are used. For example, if the photo showing no computer equipment at all were presented as a depiction of the Orlando courtroom, which it is, then the excision of all the computer equipment probably would be unfair.

Documents

Presentation software provides enormous flexibility for lawyers in the way they display documents for the fact-finder, whether judge or jury. Documents can be cropped and resized in the same way as photographs. One standard and fair way that documents are presented by experienced lawyers anchors the viewer by showing the whole document and its exhibit number, and then presents the enhancement of the document that calls attention to its important part.

For example, the document on the left was created by an expert to record certain conditions in a structure that he examined. The document is fairly busy, and difficult to explain to a lay person. This document may be a "writing" under Rule 1001(1) because it has handwritten numbers on it, although it is in fact a prepared standard diagram (that would not qualify as a "writing") that has been annotated. This is typical of a large class of documents that benefit from enhancement and specialized display. In most cases, as here, it is not determinative whether the document is found to be a writing

The expert wants to explain his notations about the area numbered 7. The usual way to do that would be to put the document on a slide and display it with its exhibit number, as shown on the right top. Then the relevant portion is "called out" by enlarging it and connecting the enlargement with lines showing the place, in the original document, from which it was taken, as shown on the right bottom.

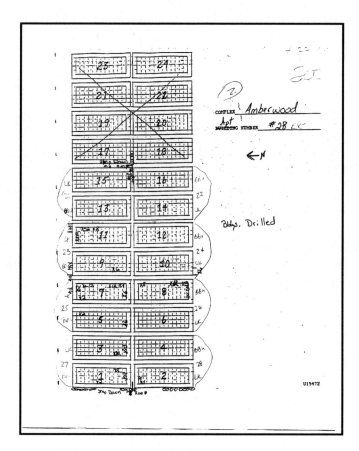

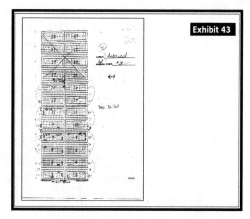

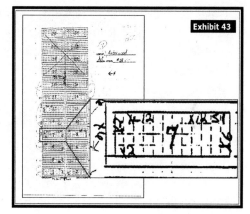

An issue may arise if counsel elects to show just the portion of the document that the witness is about to explain. The slide now looks like this when it comes up on the screen.

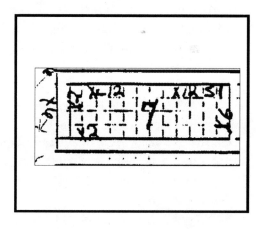

Opposing counsel may object because what is being shown to the jury is just a part of the document. There typically are three parts to an objection argument about a display that contains just a segment of a document.

First, counsel will argue that the document is a writing and, under Rule 106, the entire document should be displayed and not just a part of it. Rule 106 includes a fairness standard so, regardless of whether the document is a writing, it is probably treated the same way when the objection is raised. Counsel may urge that without the whole document in view, there is a danger of confusing or misleading the jury. That is not an insignificant problem. Jurors who are not accustomed to dealing with the kind of paper records at issue in the case may have trouble focusing on segments of documents. By the time they figure out what is being shown, the testimony has already passed to another point.

Easy Tech: Cases and Materials on Courtroom Technology
© The National Institute for Trial Advocacy

Second, counsel may argue that this excerpt is intended to limit cross-examination. This is an argument under Rule 611(a). If the only exhibit available to show on the screen is a portion of the document, then the cross-examiner cannot use the same mode (that is, an enlargement on the screen) as the direct examiner did. In this case, the cross-examiner is limited to the paper copy of the record which may be much less effective than the big screen image. There are some obvious ways around this problem. Effective preparation is one, so that the cross-examiner has digital versions of all the documents. Using the evidence camera to display the paper copy of the entire document on the large screen and zoom in on the relevant portion is another. However, it certainly is true that in direct examination counsel would not normally be allowed to approach the witness with a scissored up portion of a paper copy of a document just to bamboozle an opponent. Using just a portion of a document on a digital exhibit is about the same thing.

If the standard method is used, with the whole document displayed, it is a simple operation for opposing counsel to use that slide, with or without the callout, for cross examination and this problem is obviated. Just a basic knowledge of presentation software on the part of anyone on the trial team will allow instant enlargement of other portions of the document, competing callouts, and emphasis on whatever cross-examining counsel believes is necessary.

3.   OBJECTIONS TO ILLUSTRATIVE AIDS

The most common objections—argument, unfairness, leading, narrative testimony, facts not in evidence, and violations of the rules on opinions—are logical extensions of the objections that have been directed at large foamboard displays or other illustrative aids displayed in courtrooms in the past. When courtroom technology is being used, counsel needs to go immediately to the portion of the exhibit that may be objectionable, and trigger the proper response, as there may not be much time for thoughtful consideration. In addition, it is often necessary to "play" the illustrative aid—that is, to see it as it will unfold in the courtroom—to understand the objection in context.

A.   Argument objection

Illustrative aids used in opening statement and with lay witnesses should present facts, not argument. The objection with respect to argumentative material arises from the nature of the opening statement—creating a context for the jury's understanding—and the purpose of lay testimony—to present facts—rather than from a specific rule. For this reason, most judges regard argument as a somewhat flexible concept.

One useful axiom with respect to objections to visual displays that contain words: what is on the screen is appropriate (and not objectionable) if the lawyer or witness could say those words orally under the circumstances in which the display is introduced.

Argument most often shows up in the titles or labels for illustrative aids. Labels including adjectives and adverbs may be argumentative. Sometimes labels are displayed and then crossed out, indicating an alternative rejected or a path not taken. This may express a conclusion or argument. Labels that are opinion or argument belong only on exhibits sponsored by an expert who is qualified to give the opinion as shown by a foundation already laid.

Easy Tech: Cases and Materials on Courtroom Technology
© The National Institute for Trial Advocacy

B.   Unfairness objection

Courts use the formulation of Rule 403—danger of unfair prejudice, confusion of the issues, or misleading the jury—in dealing with objections to illustrative aids. However, there is a reasonable argument that a court has even more discretion in dealing with illustrative aids than Rule 403 provides. Rule 403 was designed for admitting or excluding evidence. Illustrative aids normally cannot qualify as evidence. They have nothing to do with whether the existence of any fact of consequence to the determination of the action is more or less probable. They are solely for the purpose of helping the witness convey information to the jury in an understandable fashion. If an illustrative aid offends Rule 403, then it should be excluded. But the court might conclude that illustrative aids can be excluded even if they do not reach the traditional threshold of Rule 403 because they are supposed to be useful and cannot serve that purpose if they do not convey useful information clearly without attendant distraction, unnecessary emphasis, or needless cumulative display.

Labels

Labels can show up over a portion of the exhibit, as a title for the exhibit, or in the margins indicating some aspect of the exhibit. Labels are the first place lawyers generally look for objectionable material.

 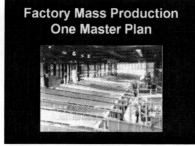 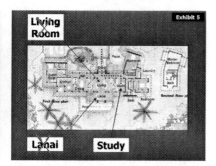

Labels that state facts should appear only after the fact is in evidence and should not misquote or mischaracterize the evidence. Sustainable objections to labels are highly dependent upon the context in which the illustrative aid is offered. Under one set of facts or at one stage of the trial the label may be objectionable and under another set of facts or later in the trial the same label may be unobjectionable.

Text treatments

Text treatments are methods for emphasizing particularly relevant portions of text embedded in a relatively long text document. These are usually boxes, underlines, circles, bold and italic type faces, and callouts. Each can be unfair if used in a way that the jury might be misled or confused about the original document. For example, words in very fine print may be enlarged and put in large bold capital letters. This may be done to give the impression that the information was emphasized in the original document when in fact it was not. This problem is largely avoided if the original document is displayed at the same time as the text treatment and standard methods for emphasis or callouts are followed.

Colors

Color usually appears on the background of the slide (behind all of the objects or writing on the slide), on an object on the slide as a way of setting off or emphasizing the content, or as a partition that makes objects on the slide appear or disappear. Examples are on the CD that accompanies this book.

Lawyers sometimes use background color to indicate the subject matter of the slide. For example, the slides that have to do with liability might have a dark blue background and the slides that have to do with damages might have a dark green background. Background color may indicate the relative importance of a slide. The most important slides may have no background color at all. Background color, even if lacking in taste or articulated purpose, is rarely objectionable.

Color used on objects or partitions may be objectionable when the purpose is to suggest linkages that may not exist in fact and for which there is no foundation. For example, a photo of a piece of equipment painted yellow may be admitted in evidence. The lawyer may then have slides that use the color yellow to suggest that other things are a part of this equipment when there is no foundation for that link. Those uses of color may be objectionable.

Unlike permanent foamboard exhibits that were their predecessors in the courtroom, slides can be changed very readily, on the spot, usually with only a few keystrokes. If there is a problem with a particular color, the slide can be retrieved, a color palette with many shades can be displayed, and the offending color can be changed instantly without changing anything else on the slide. It is an unusual case, therefore, where a party will be prejudiced by last minute changes in color required by the court.

Motion

The motion in videotapes may be objectionable when the tape is played at a speed faster or slower than normal so that the people or objects depicted on the tape are not moving at the speed they were when the tape was made. The motion in videotapes may also be objectionable if frames have been removed or edited with the effect of distorting the motion shown on the tape.

The motion in computer animations may be objectionable when there is no foundation to show that the motion depicted is accurate. For example, if an animation shows a truck approaching an intersection, and there is no foundation that the speed (motion) depicted on the screen is accurate, then under some circumstances the animation may be disqualified.

The motion in individual slides shown in a courtroom is usually one of three types.

- A *transition* is the motion that you see on the screen when the lawyer moves from one slide to the next. For example, the new slide may appear out of a tiny point at the center of the screen and expand to fill the entire screen, or it may fly in from the left margin of the screen, or horizontal blinds may close to reveal the slide. Transitions are usually unhelpful (because they can distract focus) but not objectionable.

Easy Tech: Cases and Materials on Courtroom Technology
© The National Institute for Trial Advocacy

- An *animation* is the motion that you see on the screen when an object appears on the slide. For example, a slide may have a title, a photograph, and some arrows or labels explaining the photograph. All of these objects may be on the slide when it first appears, or they may be "revealed" one at a time. When objects are revealed, they may zoom out, fly in, or have other motion associated with their appearance. Animations, while often annoying, are usually not objectionable. Occasionally an animation suggests that one thing came from or originated in another and is unfair for that reason.

- A *morph* is a motion that turns one thing into another. For example, a description in a document may morph into a photo of the thing described. The words meld together into a blob that gradually transforms itself into the photo. Morphs are usually done for a purpose that, if it has no foundation already presented, makes them objectionable.

The motions that appear on slides are produced by a set of tools that comes with presentation software. Any one of a long list of motions can be applied to any slide or any object on the slide very easily, indeed almost automatically. Sometimes motion is included on a slide for no reason other than the software made it possible and it was fun to do. Lawyers who have only recently begun to use these displays or overeager consultants may include motion where none is necessary, or worse, distracting from the message sought to be conveyed. Suspicious opposing counsel may see unfairness where there is merely lack of taste or good sense. In any case, motion that has been added to a slide can be turned off readily (a few keystrokes) without affecting anything else on the slide.

Sound

The sound on videotapes may be objectionable when speech is being recorded and the speech is hearsay that does not qualify for an exception under the rules.

The sound in computer animations may be objectionable when there is no foundation to show that the sound is accurate.

The sound in individual slides shown in a courtroom is usually produced by the same kind of tools described above with respect to motion. The standard sounds provided by the software include typing, telephone rings, glass breaking, applause, doorbell rings, camera clicks, cash register rings, chimes, drive by, drum roll, explosion, gunshot, screeching brakes, and whoosh. It is rare that any of these contribute usefully to a jury's understanding as they are all manufactured sounds that have nothing to do with the facts of the case. Sounds that have been added to a slide can be turned off very easily (a few keystrokes) without affecting anything else on the slide.

Position

Presentation software tools make it possible to position photos and other images anywhere in relation to one another. One can "flip" any image so as to make it appear as it would from the opposite side.

example   elpmaxe   ǝldɯɐxǝ

Images can be "rotated" to angles that are different from real life.

example   example

Images or objects may be overlapped on the slide when in real life they could not be in that position. Any of these positioning techniques can create an objectionable display because the purported goal of helping the jury to understand the witness's testimony or the information being presented by the witness is not achieved in a fair manner and results in nothing more than persuasion on irrelevant grounds.

Intervals

Time lines are frequently used in cases in which a sequence of dates or times are important to the case theory. Most time lines include intervals, marked off in some way, representing the amount of time that passed between events. If the intervals on the time line, when measured, do not accurately (that is, proportionally) represent the amount of time that actually passed, then there may be an objection based on presenting misleading and possibly confusing information to the jury.

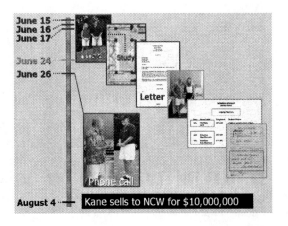

In the example on the left, the dates June 15, June 16, June 17, June 24, June 26, and August 4 are important to the case. In this case, a business broker is suing to collect a fee and her case theory is that her actions were instrumental in the sale of a business. The time line shows the actions. But the intervals shown on the time line are not exactly proportional to the amount of time that passed between one event and another. The intervals between June 15 and June 26 are reasonably accurate but, if measured, the interval between June 26 and August 4 is compressed. The unfairness objection will be based on the impression given the jurors that this time interval was shorter than it actually was.

This time line is an illustrative aid, and therefore will not be sent to the jury room during deliberations. For that reason, a relaxed standard about accuracy may be appropriate so long as the distortions are not large. In this case, it would be difficult for the designer of this slide to get all the information on one slide, with a type size that could be read. However, the use of a computer in design work makes it very easy to get time intervals exactly correct. Where the intervals are not a true representation, it might be better to indicate that with a break in the line that is the vertical axis on which the dates are indicated.

Repetition

Visual displays offer an opportunity to repeat testimony or themes, and some lawyers use this opportunity to repeat material in ways that would be objectionable if done orally by the lawyer (in a question) or by a witness. A series of slides that repeat a quote from deposition testimony is one example. Another example occurs when a lawyer introduces an animation with one eye witness and then seeks to play the entire animation with every eye witness no matter how minor the contribution of the witness's observation. The objective is to ingrain the animation in jurors' minds, perhaps before the other side's animation appears or with more frequency than the other side's animation is played. Some repetition in displays is usually tolerated, just as some repetition in testimony is allowed.

Photos

Once a photo is a digital file, it can be changed in one of three principal ways: cropping (discussed above in Section 2), resizing, and reshaping. The objection to cropping is usually to the "completeness" of the exhibit, an objection under Rule 106. The objection to resizing and reshaping is usually unfairness under Rule 403.

Resizing is a process in which the photo is made bigger or smaller, perhaps in relation to some other photo, without changing the content of the photo.

There is nothing inherently unfair about resizing a photo, but photos of different dimensions can be used to present facts unfairly. A large photo of a small object placed next to a small photo of a large object may suggest unfairly that the two are nearly the same size.

Reshaping is a process in which the photo is stretched in a north-south dimension to make the things it depicts "taller," or in an east-west direction to make the things it depicts "wider."

Easy Tech: Cases and Materials on Courtroom Technology
© The National Institute for Trial Advocacy

Reshaping is almost always inherently unfair. It is not an accurate representation of the real thing.

Every presentation software or photo editing software package provides a means to resize photos without reshaping (or distorting) them. However, it is often the case that when photos are resized they are also distorted. Lawyers often bark about deceit and fraud when they find that a photo has been distorted. In fact, distortion is usually inadvertent because the tool for resizing a photo is very similar in appearance to the tool for reshaping the photo. The fact that distortion can be inadvertent does not diminish its seriousness, but lawyers may not recognize a distorted photo that has been worked on by someone else so the fact of distortion does not always equate with intentional wrongdoing by the lawyer or the person doing the work.

C. Leading objection

The traditional objection to leading questions is directed to statements by the lawyer which suggest the desired answer to the witness. Slides may have content or markings that will lead the witness in reciting testimony. Slides that accompany expert testimony are often prepared for this very purpose, so that the expert provides an explanation that is organized and well-paced. They are less objectionable on these grounds, however, if the expert prepared the slides and determined their content. The expert is unlikely to mislead herself.

D. Narrative testimony objection

The traditional objection to narrative testimony seeks to prevent the situation where counsel is not put on notice, by the form of the question, as to potential objectionable testimony by the witness. The same can be true of a slide show that plays independent of witness foundation.

E. Facts not in evidence objection

The traditional objection in this area seeks to disqualify a question that assumes a fact not in evidence on the ground that the answer given by the witness to such a question cannot be fairly used by a jury in arriving at a decision in the case.

Slides used in the direct examination of witnesses sometimes cross into this area when a statement, photo, or other material is displayed that purports to present a fact that has not already been admitted in evidence or at least is not within the competence or knowledge of the witness with whom the slides are used.

Easy Tech: Cases and Materials on Courtroom Technology
© The National Institute for Trial Advocacy

Experts are allowed, under Rule 703, to rely on facts or data not admissible in evidence. question arises, with respect to displays used by experts to explain their opinions, whether a slide can include statements, photos, or other data not admissible in evidence as a helpful means of presenting the expert's opinion to the jury or assisting the jury in understanding the expert's opinion. Pursuant to the December 2000 changes in Rule 703, while these facts may be used as a basis for the expert's opinion, if the data or facts are not otherwise admissible, they may not, in normal circumstances, be communicated to th jury. As a result, such facts or data would not normally appear on an illustrative aid.

F.   Unsupported opinion (foundation) objection

Expert witnesses are the most frequent users of illustrative aids displayed using courtroom technology. Lawyers who prepare well for a complicated case will use jury research to identify the case themes that are likely to cause a representative jury to decide issues in the client's favor. Sometimes these themes show up in the displays that the expert sponsors even though the expert has no facts at hand or knowledge, skill, experience, training, or education that would provide a foundation for direct testimony. An objection to this kind of display is often stated as "argument," because the display is in effect arguing the client's cause.

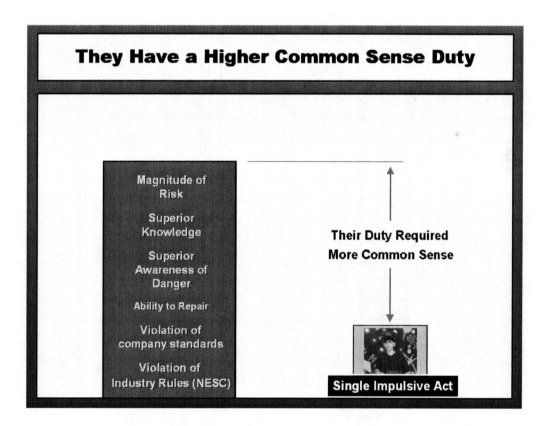

For example, here is a display that argues an ultimate issue in the case (permitted under Rule 704(a)) building on a series of opinions. The expert is prepared to testify that the defendant corporation violated industry rules, violated company standards, had the ability to do repairs that would have prevented plaintiff's injury, had an awareness of the danger, and knew the magnitude of the risk. This display builds each of these points, part by part, in a bar on the left, suggesting an amount of fault for the company. It may be unclear to opposing counsel where this is going, until the rest of the pieces of the slide are displayed showing a much smaller bar, suggesting very little fault on the part of the individual plaintiff. Finally, a title bar is displayed with the conclusion that "They (the defendant company) have a higher common sense duty." (See the CD that comes with this book to play the slide as it builds to a conclusion.) The objection to this slide likely will be lack of foundation because the expert has no basis for making a determination as to comparative fault. This objection might be obviated by removing the title bar and the commentary, and merely showing the elements of contributory negligence by the respective parties. However, implicit in the size of the bars is an opinion by the expert about the size of the contribution by each party which may be found to be inappropriate.

G. Lay opinion objection

The titles, labels, or other text on a slide used with a lay witness may be objectionable under Rule 701 if they include words or phrases that are fairly characterized as opinion or inference and do not fall within one of the two exceptions in the rule: "(a) rationally based on the perception of the witness and (b) helpful to a clear understanding of the witness' testimony or the determination of a fact in issue."

Quinlan v. Kane
Business Contracts Case

Quinlan v. Kane
Contents

Exhibits
    Exhibit 1.   Telephone message slip from Kane's secretary showing a call from Quinlan

    Exhibit 2.   Copy of a letter that Quinlan says she sent Kane confirming the commission deal dated June 16, YR-1

    Exhibit 3.   Draft letter from Quinlan to Kane dated June 16, YR-1

    Exhibit 4.   Page from Quinlan's phone log

    Exhibit 5.   Quinlan's form contract

    Exhibit 6.   Note made by Kane about Fuller call

    Exhibit 7.   Photograph of Quinlan and Kane standing together at the tee

    Exhibit 8.   Photograph of Quinlan and Kane with Kane teeing off

    Exhibit 9.   Photograph of Quinlan and Fuller at an office party talking together

    Exhibit 10.   Photograph of Quinlan and Fuller at an office party facing the camera

    Exhibit 11.   Diagram of Kane's house where the key meeting took place

    Exhibit 12.   Video clip, Quinlan deposition, pp. 35–36 (on the CD)

    Exhibit 13.   Video clip, Kane deposition, p. 22 (on the CD)

Thumbnails of Slides

Easy Tech: Cases and Materials on Courtroom Technology
© The National Institute for Trial Advocacy

PART III: Quinlan v. Kane[1]

Fact Summary

Roberta Quinlan is a business broker who specializes in the buying and selling of electronics manufacturing and sales firms. Business brokers are agents for buyers or sellers of businesses, and generally work on a commission basis. Quinlan has been a broker in the electronics industry for ten years. Kane Electronics was a family-owned chain of retail electronics outlets located throughout the State of Nita in twenty-six locations. Its president, founder, and sole shareholder was Brian Kane.

On August 4, YR-1,[2] Kane Electronics was sold to Nita Computer World , a national retailer of computers and other electronic business equipment, for $10 million of Nita Computer World stock. Roberta Quinlan claims that she served as the broker for this transaction and that she had an agreement with Brian Kane to do so. She claims that the agreement was reached during a business meeting held at Kane's house on June 16, YR-1, and was set out in a confirming letter that she mailed to Kane the next day, June 17; she also maintains that she contacted Cliff Fuller of Nita Computer World on behalf of Kane Electronics and was responsible for putting Nita Computer World and Kane together, which is what business brokers do. She has sued Kane for $300,000, 3 percent of the closing value of Kane Electronics, per her agreement with Kane.

Kane and Quinlan have known each other for about ten years, mainly as golf partners. Kane admits that he decided to sell his business in early June and that he told Quinlan of his decision during a round of golf on June 15. Kane admits he invited Quinlan to his house the next day to talk about the sale of his business. Kane admits he had several conversations with Quinlan about the possible sale of his company over the years, but he says they were all preliminary and brainstorming in nature. Kane denies there was an agreement between him and Quinlan for her to act as his agent. He denies ever receiving a confirming letter of agreement from Quinlan. He admits that when he was first contacted by phone by Cliff Fuller of Nita Computer World on June 26, YR-1, Fuller said he had been referred by Roberta Quinlan. He also admits that he did not know Fuller or of Nita Computer World's interest in his company before the Fuller phone call. Kane maintains he negotiated his own deal with Nita Computer World and does not owe Quinlan a commission.

---

1. The *Quinlan v. Kane* case is adapted from *Problems in Trial Advocacy*, © NITA 1996, by Bocchino and Beskind. An earlier version was created under this name by Bocchino and Beskind incorporating prior NITA teaching materials.

2. NITA uses a convention for dates as follows: YR-0 (this year); YR-1 (last year); YR-2 (two years ago), and so on. Students should use the actual year in working on the exercises.

DEPOSITION SUMMARY OF ROBERTA QUINLAN

My name is Roberta Quinlan. I am forty-eight years old and a lifelong resident of Nita City. I am married to William Feldman, who is a partner with the law firm of Parker & Gould in Nita City. We have two children, who are grown and on their own. I have both a BS and an MBA in business from Nita University. I began my career as a business broker once the kids were in middle school. My job is to put buyers and sellers of businesses together and help them reach sales agreements. Over the past fifteen years I have developed an expertise in companies and businesses involved in the electronics industry, both manufacturers and retailers of these products.

I have known Brian Kane for about ten years. We met in YR-10 when he asked me to play in a mixed foursome golf tournament with him at the Rolling Green Golf Club where we both are members. We are both avid players, and since that time, have regularly entered tournaments together as well as playing together socially. I have played since college. Even though Brian took up the game later in life, he is a natural athlete and fierce competitor, so we make a very good team and have been quite successful. These photos you have shown me, marked Exhibit 7 and Exhibit 8, are of Brian and me playing in the club championship round in the early summer last year before all this happened.

About five years ago Brian, who is now in his early fifties, started talking to me about possibly selling his business, Kane Electronics. Of course I already knew all about his business, including that he started it on a shoestring in YR-30 after working for Business Machines Incorporated for a few years, and that he had expanded to twenty-six retail outlets throughout the state of Nita. He too knew about my business and my expertise in the electronics industry. These conversations usually occurred either on the golf course or at lunch after our game. He seemed really torn between his love for his work and a strong feeling of guilt at not spending more time with his family.

On June 15, YR-1, Brian told me during a round of golf that he had finally decided to sell his business. I knew by then that he and his wife were having troubles, and he told me he desperately wanted to be able to spend more time with his family and get his marriage back together. I told him I would be pleased to discuss the sale and give him some advice on how to proceed. As I said, Brian knew all about my business, but there was no talk of retaining me at that point. Instead, he asked that I come by his house the next day, which was a Sunday, so that we could talk more about the sale of his business.

I got to his house about noon. We immediately went to the study and met for about four hours. We first talked about the value of the company. He had already obtained appraisals and based on those said that he hoped to get somewhere in the neighborhood of $8 to $10 million for his business. Based on the appraisals of his company and my knowledge of the industry, I told him that $8 million was low and that $10 million was a realistic goal for the sale. We then talked about the possible forms such a sale could take. I explained that because he was the sole owner of the company, the sale could be accomplished by selling all of the stock to the buyer for cash, by selling all of the assets of his company to the buyer for cash, by exchanging his stock for shares of stock in a corporate buyer, or by some combination of these methods. As it turned out, his preference was to exchange his stock for stock of the buying company if he could find a growing company as a buyer.

Easy Tech: Cases and Materials on Courtroom Technology
© The National Institute for Trial Advocacy

1. Q: As I understand it, you talked with Mr. Kane at his house in June of last

2. year, not at his office?

3. A: Yes, he wanted to meet right away on Sunday, so he suggested his home

4. which was more convenient for both of us.

5. Q: The two of you discussed various options on how he might sell his business?

6. A: Among other things, yes.

7. Q: What else did you talk about?

8. A: As I said, we went over the appraisals and my advice on the appropriate

9. selling price. We also talked about what I would charge as a brokerage fee.

10. Q: Who brought up the topic of fees?

11. A: I did. I told Brian that the range of fees for a deal such as what he was

12. interested in was 3 to 5 percent, depending upon the level of involvement by the broker.

13. Q: What did he say to that?

14. A: Nothing really, I think we just moved on to another topic.

15. Q: What was that topic?

16. A: We talked about the kind of buyer we would be looking for—stable, on the rise,

17. that sort of thing. I told him I had a lot of contacts in the industry and I was sure I could

18. find an appropriate buyer.

19. Q: What was his reaction?

20. A: He said, "I'm aware of your reputation Roberta." I assured him that I would do some

21. checking around on his behalf that next week. At that point, Brian's wife came in and

22. reminded him of a social engagement and we cut our meeting short. As I was leaving,

23. I told him I'd call him next week or so. I believed that Nita Computer World was a potential

24. buyer and intended to check that out.

1. Q: When at his house, you did not tell Mr. Kane that you had someone in mind

2. who might be interested, did you?

3. A: No. I didn't want to raise premature expectations.

4. Q: Did Mr. Kane ask you to check with your contacts in the industry?

5. A: No, but he didn't say not to.

6. Q: And he didn't say that you should do some checking either, did he?

7. A: Not in so many words, no.

8. Q: Did you believe that Mr. Kane had contracted for your services at that point?

9. A: Not formally, that's why I wrote him that same day.

10. Q: But he never said "You're hired" or "I want to hire you to help sell my

11. business," or anything like that, did he?

12. A: Brian never said we had a deal explicitly, but he also didn't tell me not to

13. go forward on his behalf, either.

As I was leaving, I told Brian that given the excellent shape his company was in, I felt as though we could proceed fairly quickly to a desirable conclusion. I knew that Nita Computer World was actively acquiring smaller retail outlets and thought that they were a potential buyer for Brian's company. I was familiar with Nita Computer World because my husband had handled a number of acquisitions for them in late YR-2 and early YR-1.

While I would have preferred it, the fact is we didn't sign a contract that day, but it was clear to me we had a deal. When I got home that evening I wrote and mailed a letter to Brian setting out our agreement. The letter marked as Exhibit 2 is dated June 16, YR-1. I kept a copy for my files. The other letter in my files to Kane, also dated June 16, YR-1, and marked as Exhibit 3, is a copy of my first draft of my letter to Kane. After I read it over, I realized it wasn't accurate as to our agreement so I wrote and sent Exhibit 2. I don't even know why I kept Exhibit 3—I should have discarded it with the original. I also talked with my husband that night about Nita Computer World as a possible purchaser, and he suggested I call Cliff Fuller, general counsel at Nita Computer World, whom I had met recently at a social event at my husband's firm. Exhibits 9 and 10 are photos of Cliff and me at that event.

The document you have shown me with the heading "Broker Agreement" at the top, Exhibit 5, is a form contract that I usually use in signing up clients. My husband's law firm prepared this for me so that the terms of the agreement with the client would be clear. In Brian's case, given our relationship as friends, I decided to use a letter instead of the form contract. I don't remember any other recent deal in which I used a letter, but my relationship with Brian outside of business was unique among recent clients. I regard a letter as being just as good as a contract.

When I didn't hear back from Brian wanting to change our agreement as spelled out in my letter, I arranged that next week for Cliff Fuller to call Brian. Exhibit 4 is my phone log for June 24, YR-1. It shows that call, and the call I made to Brian telling him to expect a call from Cliff Fuller. I keep a log on my computer that I fill in as I'm making phone calls, and this is a printout of that log for that date. While I didn't actually talk with Brian that day, I did leave a message on his voice mail saying to expect a call from Fuller. I tried to call him again later that day, as shown by my phone log, but this time I spoke with his secretary who said, after checking, that Brian wasn't in. I decided not to leave another message other than that I had called.

I found out through my husband that Cliff Fuller did call Brian and that there was mutual interest right off the bat. I called Brian several times after that, but he didn't return any of my calls. No, I don't have phone logs for those calls. I have looked for logs but couldn't find them. I must have called from someplace other than the office, perhaps on my cell phone. I am told they started working on a deal immediately and that the negotiations went smoothly. I was not involved at all in these negotiations, but I was responsible for putting Fuller and Kane together. That's what a broker does. It's for that reason that I deserve the minimum fee that I set out in my contract letter to Brian. Usually the broker will be more involved in the negotiations, but I have had other deals like this where the principals do their own negotiations. It's for that reason that once Kane and Fuller were talking I didn't insert myself into the proceedings. I was always available if needed. I did not have to do a lot of work, obviously, but in my business it's often the work you've done over the years and whom you know, not how much work you do on the particular assignment, that makes or breaks a deal. Brian Kane got top dollar for his business, consistent with my advice to him, and if I had not called Cliff Fuller the deal would never have happened.

Now Brian doesn't want to pay me for what I've earned. I know he claims he never got my letter, but I mailed it out myself on my stationery, and it was never returned to me by the post office, so I'm sure he got it. He had plenty of time to call or write or fax me calling off the deal, but he never did. It's unfortunate that this has happened, and that I have to sue a former friend to get the fee I deserve, but Brian should pay me what I'm owed.

I have read this deposition and it is complete and accurate.

Roberta Quinlan

_____
Roberta Quinlan
12/28/YR-1

DEPOSITION SUMMARY OF BRIAN KANE

My name is Brian Kane. I am fifty-four years old and have lived here in Nita City all my life. My wife Elvira and I are currently separated and she has our three beautiful teenage daughters living with her. After I graduated from Nita University in YR-33, I worked three years for Business Machines Incorporated at their Brookline, Massachusetts facility before deciding to set out on my own in the retail electronics business. I moved back to Nita City, and with the help of some friends and family and a bank, I scraped together enough money to open my first retail electronics store in YR-30. Through a lot of hard work and good timing, the business expanded over the years to where I ended up with twenty-six locations all over the state. I was the president, founder, and sole shareholder of the company during all the years before I sold it.

For the first fifteen years of being in business, my life was my business. I had little time for outside activities, even dating. Then in YR-18 I met Elvira, a customer who wanted to register a complaint with the "boss" of the company. We married not long afterwards. Bianca, our first child, was born in YR-17. Rachel was born in YR-15, and Terry in YR-13. Not long after Rachel's birth, I decided I needed something to take my mind off of the grind of work, so I took up golf, and it became a real passion.

It was through golf that I met Roberta Quinlan. After I joined Rolling Green Golf Club in about YR-15, I remember seeing her on the driving range hitting balls and was very impressed. She could really hit a golf ball. Not long after, I asked her if she would be my partner in a mixed foursome tournament and that started a long friendship centered around golf. She was a lot of fun to play with and had the same kind of competitive spirit that I have, which resulted in a number of trophies for us both. Exhibits 7 and 8 are photos of Roberta and me at the club.

I was also impressed with Roberta's knowledge of business. We often talked about both our businesses and I would pick her brain with ideas I had for expansion and the occasional thought of selling my business so I could do something else. Over the years, talk of my selling out was more frequent as I became more disenchanted with being unable to spend quality time with my family and Elvira's discontent with that fact. Like the many other real estate and business brokers that I had dealt with over the years, however, Roberta tended to be a little too aggressive in her own self-promotion. My experience with brokers over the years has been that they are at best a necessary evil, but I never have liked the way they hit you up and try to push you into giving them business.

In early YR-1 I started having serious problems in my marriage. I began to reevaluate my life and decided I had been spending far too much time at the office, and not enough with my family. My daughters only had another few years before they would be out of the house and in college, and if there was to be any chance of salvaging my marriage, I needed to make some changes. By May I had committed in my own mind to sell out. I hired a couple of appraisers to value my company, did some research on my own, made a few calls to people I knew in the industry, and put out feelers. Although I hadn't been successful as of then, my business was in good shape, in an expanding market, and I was sure I could find a buyer in time.

Easy Tech: Cases and Materials on Courtroom Technology
© The National Institute for Trial Advocacy

The next time I saw Roberta, at a golf game in mid-June, I told her of my decision. She got all excited and wanted to talk about nothing else the rest of the day. She urged me to let her broker the deal, wanted to spend a few hours meeting with me after our round of golf, and on and on. Just to get her to calm down and let me enjoy the golf game, I told her we could talk about it the next day at my house. Even though I had no intention of hiring her because I had decided to do this deal myself, I still felt as though I might learn something talking with her and I didn't want to hurt her feelings by abruptly cutting her off and telling her she had no chance of getting this business. I now regret that decision.

When she came over the next day, June 16, a Sunday, we went straight to my study, which is where I work when I am at home. Exhibit 11 is a diagram of the layout of my house and it shows the study where we met. Roberta was more than her usual aggressive self in trying to get me to sign on the dotted line, so to speak, and make her my agent for this deal. I kept putting her off, saying I had to think it all over. I must admit that I was trying to learn as much as I could from her about how she thought the deal might be structured and how she saw things working out best for me. But I had picked her brain for years on business deals without ever hiring her. I definitely did not hire her at this meeting. We just talked. There were many options discussed. At one point I do remember that she told me that her fee for helping me would only be 3–5 percent and I tried to make her feel as though I thought that was very reasonable. Of course, what I was really thinking was that by handling the sale myself, with the help of my lawyers of course, I would be saving anywhere from $250,000 to $500,000 by bypassing a broker such as Roberta.

Page 22

1. Q: Why didn't you just flat out tell Mrs. Quinlan that you didn't want her

2. as your agent on this sale?

3. A: I didn't want to seem rude or harsh with my long-time friend and golf partner.

4. Q: But didn't she tell you she'd be looking around for a buyer for your business?

5. A: Yes, but I never told her she should. I thought that was just all part of her sales pitch.

6. Q: Did you tell her not to?

7. A: No, I didn't.

8   Q: Did you encourage her to keep a lookout?

9. A: No, I didn't actively encourage her.

10. Q: What did you do then?

11.   A: I learned long ago in business to keep my options open. I thought, who knows

12.   what she might come up with, so I said nothing.

13.   Q: What did you think she'd do based on this meeting?

14.   A: Well, had I thought about it, I guess I should have known Roberta, as aggressive

15.   as she is in business, would try to find someone to buy my business and get the

16.   sizeable commission for the deal, but I never hired her to do that for me. She took

17.   that upon herself without my approval.

Fortunately, my wife came into the study and reminded me of a social engagement. I was very glad to end that meeting with Roberta. First she was very pushy, then she tried to guilt trip me into hiring her, talking on and on about her contacts in the industry. That's what they all say, you know. It felt like someone trying to get you to change phone companies, and I wanted no part of it.

I remember telling my secretary, Margaret Edmondson, the next day that if Roberta Quinlan called, she was to say I wasn't in. I really didn't like dealing with this side of Roberta's personality, and I was having enough trouble with one woman in my life and didn't need Roberta hassling me too. Exhibit 1 is a telephone slip with my secretary's handwriting on it. I don't remember getting this, but it is consistent with my instructions.

I understand that Roberta claims to have sent me a so-called confirming letter after our meeting. There was nothing to confirm, and besides I never received any such letter from her. Had I received such a letter, I am sure I would have replied instantly telling her as nicely as I could that I didn't want her services for this transaction. Having since read the copy of the letter she claims to have sent (Exhibit 2), I wonder how one can have a deal when even the commission is totally loosey-goosey.

In late June I got a call from Cliff Fuller, the general counsel at Nita Computer World. I didn't know him at all, nor did I have any idea that they might be interested in my company. Exhibit 6 is a note I made about Fuller's call. I did know the company, however, as a major player in the electronics field, and recognized that they were large enough to be able to pay top dollar for my business. Cliff told me in that first call that he had been told by Roberta to call me. It never occurred to me that Roberta would expect to be compensated for this phone call. We arranged to meet for lunch. I don't recall whether Fuller suggested that Roberta join us. He might have, but there was no reason for her to be there. Once Cliff and I talked, I handled everything myself just as I had planned and after some back and forth and meetings with the lawyers, we arrived at a mutually agreeable arrangement whereby Nita Computer World bought my company in exchange for $10 million of their stock. We probably had ten meetings in all, all without Roberta. It's true that Roberta discussed that form of sale with me, but in the end, it was my tax lawyers who persuaded me to close the deal in that form. The deal closed on August 4. I was ecstatic. Finally I would have time to be with my kids, and try to make things right with Elvira, and then this lawsuit got filed.

It's not the money that she's asking for that troubles me so much; it's the principle of the thing. If I had wanted Roberta to be my agent, then I would have hired her and signed an agreement specifically setting out our arrangement. That's how I have always done business, in writing. That's the only safe way to proceed I quickly learned some thirty years ago. I never agreed to hire her; instead she's trying to foist herself on me and my company and I don't like it. And this has ruined a perfectly good golf team, too.

I have read this deposition and it is complete and accurate.

Brian Kane

Brian Kane
12/29/YR-1

DEPOSITION SUMMARY OF CLIFF FULLER

My name is Clifford Fuller. I am forty-four years old, my wife's name is Maggie, and I have one child, who is in high school. I am a lifelong resident of Nita, and I graduated from Nita Law School. I live in the same house that I grew up in, and my father, who is quite old now, lives with us. My first job out of law school was with the firm of Parker & Gould, where for many years I worked with William Feldman, the husband of the plaintiff in this case. I didn't know his wife Roberta very well because she only came to a few office functions during the years I was at the firm. Exhibits 9 and 10 are photos taken at one of those functions. I never knew much about her other than she worked as a business broker after their kids got older, and she went by her maiden name of Quinlan.

About five years ago, I left the firm to take the position of general counsel with one of the firm's biggest clients, Nita Computer World. I had represented Nita Computer World in quite a few of their acquisitions during my years at the firm. It is now a very substantial company in the electronics field. In my job as general counsel, I negotiate deals for the company, make sure we are complying with state and federal regulations, and advise the officers and managers. I also manage our litigation with outside counsel.

In late June of YR-1, Roberta Quinlan called me at the office. After exchanging pleasantries, she told me that an old friend and client, Brian Kane of Kane Electronics, was interested in selling his business. She told me a few basic facts about the business, probably the gross revenues, number of locations, and things like that. I don't remember specifically what she said, but she certainly sounded knowledgeable. I know she mentioned that Kane had appraisals for his company in the $10 to $12 million range, which initially seemed reasonable. She said she had heard that Nita Computer World was acquiring businesses of this kind, and she asked me if our company might be interested in such a purchase. I told her we definitely might be, but of course, we have a lot of hoops to jump through when we are considering an acquisition. She talked about a deal for stock, and said that Kane was interested in being acquired by a growing company. There is no doubt that she spoke as if she was the broker for Kane Electronics, and I assumed she was.

She told me to call Brian Kane directly if we decided we were interested and gave me his office and home phone numbers. This was a little odd because usually brokers like to make the introduction. After talking with the necessary people at our company, I called Mr. Kane on June 26 and we set up a lunch to talk things over. I know that I told him that I was calling at the suggestion of Roberta Quinlan. I also asked if Roberta would be joining us for lunch and he said he'd see if she was available. Kane and I hit it off right away. We talked about a deal for stock, and it was clear to me that we were both on the same track. I later introduced him to our president and soon after we all met with their lawyers. After some back and forth, there were probably ten meetings in all, we arrived at a price and Nita Computer World purchased Kane Electronics for $10 million of our stock. The deal closed in early August. We have been very happy with this purchase and I thought we got a great deal.

Yes, I guess I was a little surprised that I never either heard from or saw Roberta Quinlan after that initial phone call. I thought for sure, as the broker, she would at least sit in on some of the

Easy Tech: Cases and Materials on Courtroom Technology
© The National Institute for Trial Advocacy

meetings that led up to our agreement with Mr. Kane. I have no firsthand knowledge of what their arrangement was; all I can go on is what Ms. Quinlan told me over the phone. I must say, Mr. Kane never mentioned her at all in all of our dealings. Yes, I do remember telling Mr. Kane, when we first spoke, that his broker had called me, and I identified her by name. He said he often played golf with her, and we went on to talk about the deal. He didn't seem surprised that I mentioned her. He didn't say anything to suggest she was his broker, but he didn't say anything to suggest she wasn't his broker either.

Kane handled the deal basically by himself, only using lawyers to close the deal. He seemed to have made up his mind what he wanted to do, and to me at least it did not appear that he was relying on anyone's advice. He had lawyers working on the papers, but they were just writing up what he decided. He's kind of a quiet person. He doesn't talk much. But he was a good person to negotiate with. Once he said he'd do something, he didn't change his mind or try to renegotiate the terms.

I have read this deposition and it is complete and accurate.

_____
Clifford Fuller
12/27/YR-1

Easy Tech: Cases and Materials on Courtroom Technology
© The National Institute for Trial Advocacy

DEPOSITION SUMMARY OF MARGARET EDMONDSON

My name is Margaret Edmondson, but I am usually called Peg. I am forty-four years old, married with two children, and live at 1445 Old City Way in Nita City. Until August of YR-1, I was the Secretary/Administrative Assistant to Brian Kane of Kane Electronics. I now work as an office manager for Nita Computer World, the company that bought Mr. Kane's business. He was instrumental in my getting my current job. In addition, when Mr. Kane sold his business, I received a bonus of $50,000 which he said was for my years of hard work on his behalf. Mr. Kane gave bonuses to about 20 of us who had been with him for many years. I don't know what others received. I also took from the company a retirement plan that I had paid into together with contributions from Kane Electronics. Although I no longer work for Mr. Kane, it is fair to say that I remain loyal to him. He has always been a good and fair employer for me and everyone else who worked for him.

I started work with Mr. Kane in YR-26. At that point Kane Electronics was just one store in Nita City, although the year I started we opened up two other stores in other parts of the city. I was fresh out of high school where I had taken a business curriculum and I was hired to assist Mr. Kane's secretary, Nancy Owens. When Nancy moved with her family out of state in YR-21, I became Mr. Kane's secretary. Over time, as my responsibilities grew with the business, I got the title of Administrative Assistant, although I always continued to do Mr. Kane's secretarial work. In that capacity my job duties included Mr. Kane's word processing, his filing, his correspondence, and answering his phones and talking messages when Mr. Kane was unavailable.

Kane Electronics grew to a chain of twenty-five stores throughout the State of Nita during the time I worked there. I was always located at our main office that was originally in the downtown Nita City store. Later, in YR-10, we moved to an office complex Mr. Kane built called Kane Plaza. Mr. Kane was in the office at least three days a week, although he was constantly on the road visiting our other stores. Honestly, I don't know how he kept up the pace for as long as he did.

Mr. Kane was very successful in his business but it took a toll on his personal life. His wife and three daughters are extremely important to him and I know he felt guilty about not spending more time with them. His wife would frequently call for him at the office and would be irritated if he wasn't there or if I wasn't able to put her through because he wasn't taking calls. I also know that she resented his playing golf, which was his only recreation, because of the time it took, especially when he played in tournaments with Roberta Quinlan. Mr. Kane started to talk about selling out his business about six or seven years ago, more frequently as time went on.

In the Spring of YR-1, Mr. Kane definitely decided to sell his business. He had a conversation with me about it, and was apologetic about it, but said that he had to try to save his marriage for the sake of his children. I told him that he was right to sell, that his children had to come first. I think I was the first person in the company to know about his decision because I was the one who arranged for appraisals and the like, so Mr. Kane wanted me to know what was going

Easy Tech: Cases and Materials on Courtroom Technology
© The National Institute for Trial Advocacy

on. I remember when the appraisals came in. He hired two different appraisers to be sure. As it turned out, both appraisals put a range of valuation for the company at a little over $8 million as a low and a little over $10 million at the high end. Mr. Kane was very pleased with the appraisals. He commented to me about the appraisals that he hoped they were accurate; that he would sell in a minute for $8 million. I asked him what the process would be and he told me that he intended to handle the sale himself, which was typical of Mr. Kane. He often said that, "If you want something done right then you should do it yourself."

I was unhappy to hear about this lawsuit by Roberta Quinlan. In a way it was my fault. The weekend after Mr. Kane got the appraisals, I knew he had a golf tournament with Quinlan as his partner. I knew she was some sort of business broker and I suggested that Mr. Kane get some tips from her; after all, they had been friends for years. I know they spoke because the next Monday Mr. Kane told me that Quinlan was being very aggressive trying to get him to hire her and that he didn't want to take her calls. He said, "You know me, Peg, this is my business. I have to have control." Sure enough she called that day or the next, and per Mr. Kane's instruction, I took a message. Exhibit 1 is that message. Shortly thereafter, Mr. Kane got a call from a Mr. Fuller at Nita Computer World. Mr. Kane was real excited about the lunch meeting they scheduled and told me that he might have lucked out and the sale might happen quicker than even he had hoped. He also thanked me for suggesting that he talk to Quinlan because apparently Mr. Fuller heard about Mr. Kane's company being available from her, or at least so he said. After the meeting he was even more optimistic.

Mr. Kane and Mr. Fuller met together several times themselves and over time others were involved including the lawyers to finalize the deal. Roberta Quinlan never participated in any of those meetings to my knowledge, and because I was the one to check everyone's schedule for meetings, I'm sure I would have known if she had. And no, we never received a letter from Quinlan about her working as Mr. Kane's broker. I have never seen Exhibit 2 or 3 before, and I'm very sure about that. First, I open all of Mr. Kane's mail and if such a letter came in I would have remembered it because obviously the sale of the business was the most important thing on our agenda in that time frame. Second, I know that Mr. Kane intended to do this deal, like all the others he did, by himself, and this letter would definitely have caught my attention. Yes, that is the proper address on both Exhibits 2 and 3.

Margaret Edmondson
_____
Margaret Edmondson
12/27/YR-1

JURY INSTRUCTIONS

1. The Court will now instruct you about the law that governs this case. By your oath, you agreed to accept and follow these instructions and to apply them to the facts you find from the evidence. Any verdict in this case must be the unanimous decision of all jurors.

2. The plaintiff, Roberta Quinlan, claims that the defendant, Brian Kane, breached a contract to pay her for services as a business broker. The defendant, Brian Kane, denies that claim.

3. As the plaintiff, Roberta Quinlan has the burden of proving her claim by a preponderance of the evidence, which is the greater weight of the evidence or the evidence that you find is more believable.

4. To prevail on her claim, the plaintiff, Roberta Quinlan, must show (a) she and Brian Kane made an agreement or contract that she would perform services as a business broker, and he would pay her an agreed amount or the reasonable value of those services, (b) she performed the agreed services, and (c) he failed to pay her the amount due.

5. An agreement or contract can be formed by one or more writings, oral statements, or conduct which collectively demonstrates that each of the parties agreed to the same terms.

6. If you find that the plaintiff, Roberta Quinlan, proved her claim by a preponderance of the evidence then your verdict should be for the plaintiff, and you should determine the amount she is due as damages according to the terms of that agreement or contract.

7. If you find that the plaintiff, Roberta Quinlan, failed to prove her claim by a preponderance of the evidence, then your verdict should be for the defendant, Brian Kane.

Easy Tech: Cases and Materials on Courtroom Technology
© The National Institute for Trial Advocacy

IN THE UNITED STATES DISTRICT COURT

FOR THE DISTRICT OF NITA

ROBERTA QUINLAN,   :

               :

       Plaintiff,   :   CIVIL ACTION NO. 1298

vs.   :

               :   <u>VERDICT FORM</u>

BRIAN KANE,   :

               :

       Defendant.   :

               :

We, the jury, unanimously find:

MARK AN "X" ON THE CORRECT LINE.

IF YOUR VERDICT IS FOR THE PLAINTIFF, FILL IN AN AMOUNT THERE.

_____   For the plaintiff, Roberta Quinlan, in the amount of

                $_____.

_____   For the defendant, Brian Kane.

                   _____

                                Foreperson

Easy Tech: Cases and Materials on Courtroom Technology
© The National Institute for Trial Advocacy

EXHIBIT 1

```
╭──────────────────────────────────────╮
│   IMPORTANT MESSAGE                    │
│ For  Brian                             │
│ Day  6/24        Time  2:30      A.M.  │
│                                  P.M.  │
│ M  S. Quinlan                          │
│ Of                                     │
│ Phone   225 · 6482                     │
│ FAX   Area Code    Number    Extension │
│ MOBILE                                 │
│       Area Code    Number    Extension │
├───────────┬──────────────┬─────────────┤
│ Telephoned│✓Returned your call│ RUSH    │
│ Came to see you│ Please call │ Special attention │
│ Wants to see you│ Will call again │ Caller on hold │
├───────────┴──────────────┴─────────────┤
│ Message   Told her you                 │
│           were not in —                │
│           as per your                  │
│              instructions              │
│                                        │
│ Signed    Peg                          │
│ Universal 48023        LITHO IN U.S.A  │
╰──────────────────────────────────────╯
```

Easy Tech: Cases and Materials on Courtroom Technology
© The National Institute for Trial Advocacy

EXHIBIT 2

ROBERTA QUINLAN
Business Broker
12 Meredith Lane
Nita City, NI 99992

June 16, YR-1

Mr. Brian Kane
One Kane Plaza
P.O. Box 626
Nita City, NI 99992

Dear Brian:

It was a pleasure to visit with you this afternoon, and I write to confirm our understanding.

You, as the sole shareholder of Kane Electronics, desire to dispose of your stock holdings in the company by way of an exchange of shares of a corporation with a good investment future. If I arrange for such an exchange, which is acceptable to you, Kane Electronics will pay me a fee calculated at between 3-5 percent of the closing value to you, dependent upon my time and effort necessary on your behalf.

If I do not hear from you, I will assume that this arrangement is acceptable to you. I already have a prospect in mind and will be in touch with you in the near future.

Warm regards,

Roberta Quinlan

rq/s

COPY

EXHIBIT 3

ROBERTA QUINLAN
Business Broker
12 Meredith Lane
Nita City, NI 99992

June 16, YR-1

Mr. Brian Kane
One Kane Plaza
P.O. Box 626
Nita City, NI 99992

Dear Brian:

It was a pleasure to visit with you this afternoon concerning the sale of Kane Electronics. As I told you, I am confident that I can find an appropriate purchaser of either the assets or the stock of the company, although I understand that you are also open to an exchange of your stock in Kane for stock in a company with a good investment future.

During our conversation, we agreed that I would use my best efforts and contacts (which are many) to find a suitable purchaser of Kane Electronics. Upon consummation of any sale, regardless of its nature or form, which results from my efforts, Kane Electronics will pay me an amount to be decided upon at a later date, but in no event less than 3 percent of the net closing value to the seller.

I will be in touch with you from time to time.

Warm regards,

Roberta Quinlan

rq/s

COPY

EXHIBIT 4

ROBERTA QUINLAN
Business Broker

Outgoing Phone Log

Date	Person Called	Telephone #	Business Purpose
6/24	Cliff Fuller NCW	287-1440	Called re: potential interest in Kane Electronics. Says NCW looking to acquire companies like Kane. Thinks Kane may already be on their list of potential acquisitions. He will call Kane.
6/24	Brian Kane Kane Electronics	877-2893	Called to tell him expect call from Cliff Fuller at NCW. Left message on voice mail.
6/24	Brian Kane Kane Electronics	877-2893	Called again, Secretary claims isn't in. I hope he isn't ducking me to try to get out of our agreement (don't be paranoid)

EXHIBIT 5

BROKER AGREEMENT

AGREEMENT made this ____ day of _____, by and between Roberta Quinlan, Business Broker, 12 Meredith Lane, Nita City, NI 99992, hereinafter "broker," and _____, hereinafter "customer."

In consideration of the mutual agreements hereinafter contained and other good and valuable consideration, the sufficiency and adequacy of which are hereby acknowledged, the parties hereto agree as follows:

1. The term of this contract is six months (180 days) from the date that appears above.

2. Customer hereby retains the Broker to locate a buyer or seller as appropriate for the requirements of the Customer.

3. Broker here by undertakes to use best efforts to locate a buyer or seller as appropriate for the requirements of the Customer. Broker makes no guarantee or warranty of success with respect to any such efforts.

4. If the Broker locates a willing buyer or a willing seller as appropriate for the requirements of the Customer, the Broker has completed performance under this Agreement and is entitled to the fee described in paragraph 3.

5. Customer hereby agrees to pay to Broker a fee of ____% of the total selling price for the business, including the fair market value of any stock, stock options, warrants or other consideration of any kind, at the closing of the sale, in cash, by certified check, or by wire transfer.

6. This agreement shall inure to the benefit of, and shall be binding upon, the parties hereto and their successors and assigns. This Agreement shall be governed by the laws of the State of Nita. This Agreement may be executed in one or more counterparts, which, taken together, shall constitute the whole agreement, and there may be duplicate originals of this Agreement.

IN WITNESS WHEREOF, this Broker Agreement has been duly executed by the parties hereto as of the date first above written.

WITNESS:

_____   _____
                                          Roberta Quinlan, Broker

_____   _____
                                          Customer

EXHIBIT 6

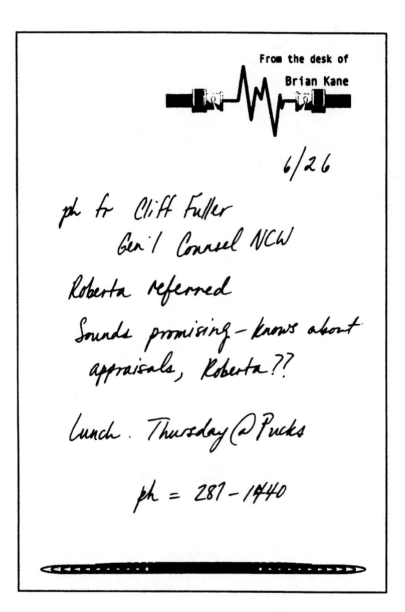

From the desk of
Brian Kane

6/26

ph fr Cliff Fuller
Gen'l Counsel NCW

Roberta referred

Sounds promising — knows about
appraisals, Roberta??

Lunch. Thursday @ Pucks

ph = 287 - 1440

EXHIBIT 7

EXHIBIT 8

EXHIBIT 9

EXHIBIT 10

EXHIBIT 11

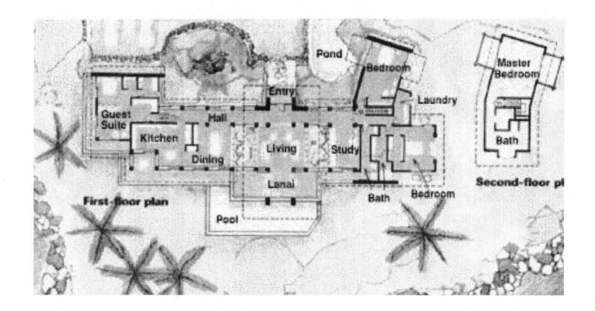

Blank Slide   **Slide 1**

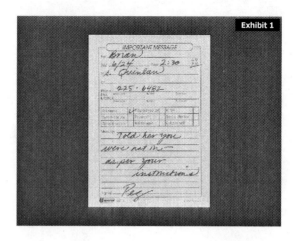

Exhibit 1   **Slide 2**

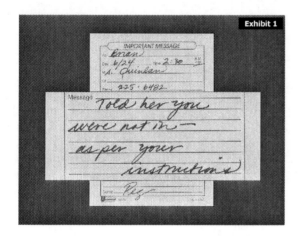

Exhibit 1   **Slide 3**

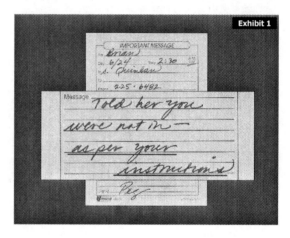

Exhibit 1   **Slide 4**

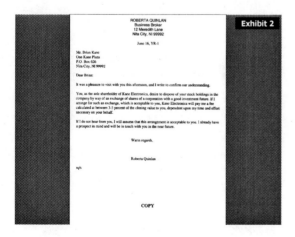

Exhibit 2   **Slide 5**

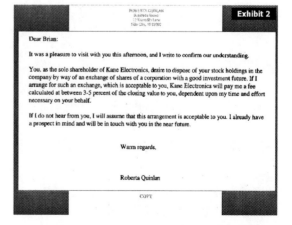

Exhibit 2   **Slide 6**

Easy Tech: Cases and Materials on Courtroom Technology
© The National Institute for Trial Advocacy

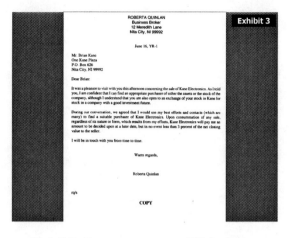

Exhibit 3   **Slide 7**

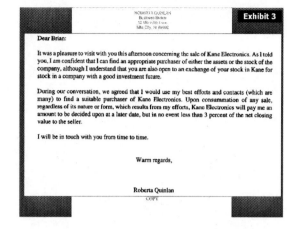

Exhibit 3   **Slide 8**

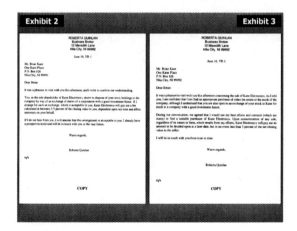

Exhibit 2 & 3   **Slide 9**

Dear Brian:

It was a pleasure to visit with you this afternoon, and I write to confirm our understanding.

You, as the sole shareholder of Kane Electronics, desire to dispose of your stock holdings in the company by way of an exchange of shares of a corporation with a good investment future. If I arrange for such an exchange, which is acceptable to you, Kane Electronics will pay me a fee calculated at between 3-5 percent of the closing value to you, dependent upon my time and effort necessary on your behalf.

If I do not hear from you, I will assume that this arrangement is acceptable to you. I already have a prospect in mind and will be in touch with you in the near future.

`Exhibit 2`

Dear Brian:

It was a pleasure to visit with you this afternoon concerning the sale of Kane Electronics. As I told you, I am confident that I can find an appropriate purchaser of either the assets or the stock of the company, although I understand that you are also open to an exchange of your stock in Kane for stock in a company with a good investment future.

During our conversation, we agreed that I would use my best efforts and contacts (which are many) to find a suitable purchaser of Kane Electronics. Upon consummation of any sale, regardless of its nature or form, which results from my efforts, Kane Electronics will pay me an amount to be decided upon at a later date, but in no event less than 3 percent of the net closing value to the seller.

I will be in touch with you from time to time.

`Exhibit 3`

Exhibit 2 & 3   **Slide 10**

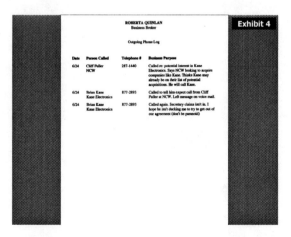

Exhibit 4   **Slide 11**

Exhibit 4   **Slide 12**

Easy Tech: Cases and Materials on Courtroom Technology
© The National Institute for Trial Advocacy

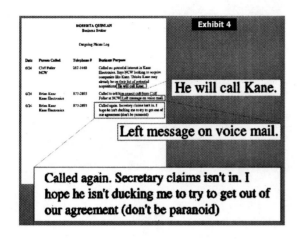

Exhibit 4   **Slide 13**

Exhibit 5   **Slide 14**

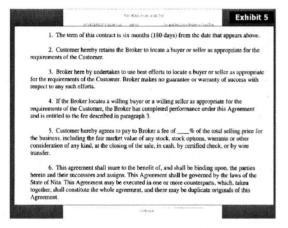

Exhibit 5   **Slide 15**

Exhibit 5   **Slide 16**

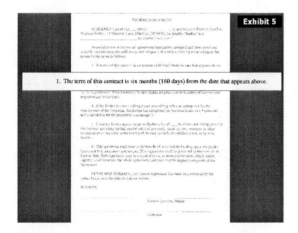

Exhibit 5   **Slide 17**

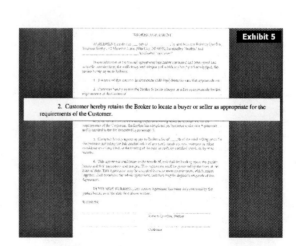

Exhibit 5   **Slide 18**

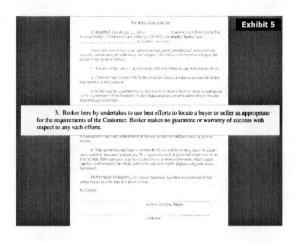

Exhibit 5   **Slide 19**

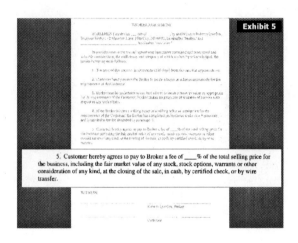

Exhibit 5   **Slide 21**

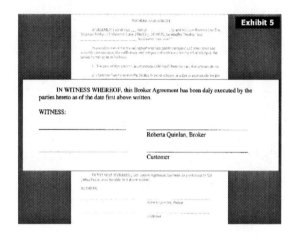

Exhibit 5   **Slide 22**

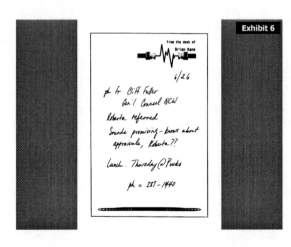

Exhibit 6   **Slide 23**

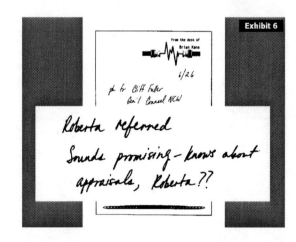

Exhibit 6   **Slide 24**

Easy Tech: Cases and Materials on Courtroom Technology
© The National Institute for Trial Advocacy

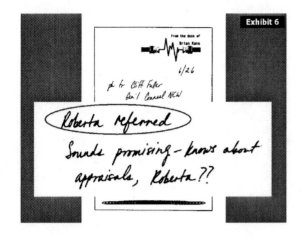

Exhibit 6   **Slide 25**

Exhibit 7   **Slide 26**

Exhibit 8   **Slide 27**

Exhibit 9   **Slide 28**

Exhibit 10   **Slide 29**

Exhibit 7 & 10   **Slide 30**

Easy Tech: Cases and Materials on Courtroom Technology
© The National Institute for Trial Advocacy

The Quinlan Connection

Exhibit 8 & 9   **Slide 31**

The Quinlan Connection

Exhibit 7–10   **Slide 32**

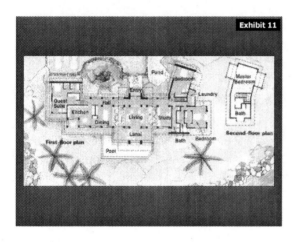

Exhibit 11   **Slide 33**

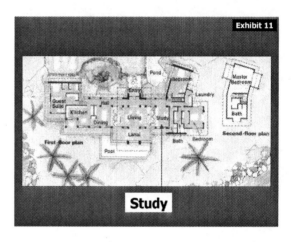

Exhibit 11   **Slide 34**

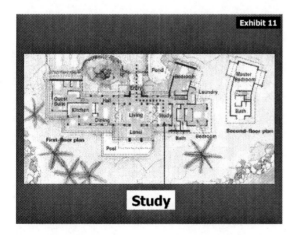

Exhibit 11   **Slide 35**

Jury Instructions   **Slide 36**

Easy Tech: Cases and Materials on Courtroom Technology
© The National Institute for Trial Advocacy

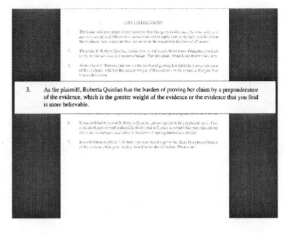

Jury Instruction 3   **Slide 37**

Jury Instruction 4   **Slide 38**

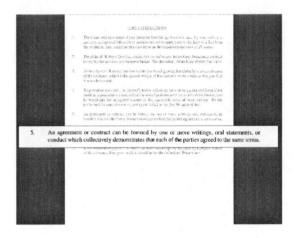

Jury Instruction 5   **Slide 39**

Verdict Form   **Slide 40**

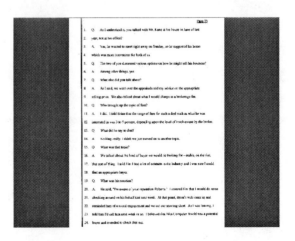

Quinlan p. 35   **Slide 41**

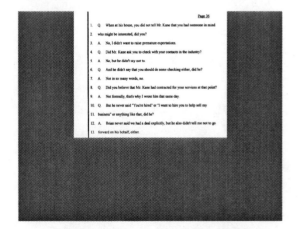

Quinlan p. 36   **Slide 42**

Quinlan video   **Slide 43**

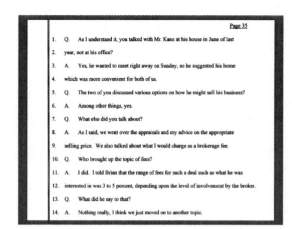

Quinlan p. 35 1–14   **Slide 44**

Quinlan video   **Slide 45**

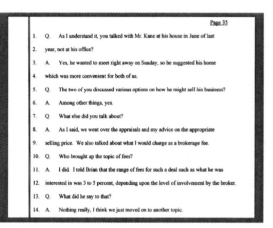

Quinlan Q & A reveal   **Slide 46**

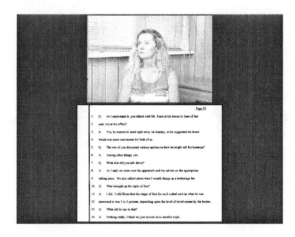

Quinlan video +   **Slide 47**

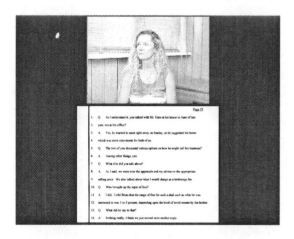

Quinlan video +   **Slide 48**

Easy Tech: Cases and Materials on Courtroom Technology
© The National Institute for Trial Advocacy

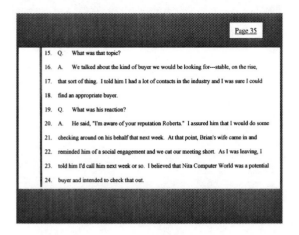

Quinlan p. 35 15–24 **Slide 49**

Quinlan video **Slide 50**

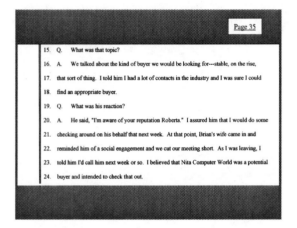

Quinlan Q & A reveal **Slide 51**

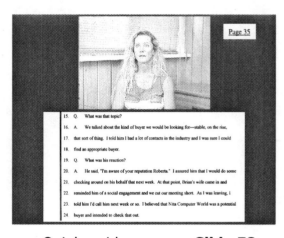

Quinlan video + **Slide 52**

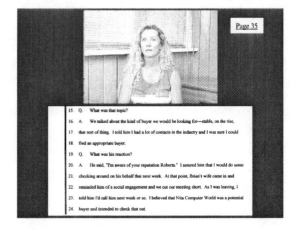

Quinlan video + **Slide 53**

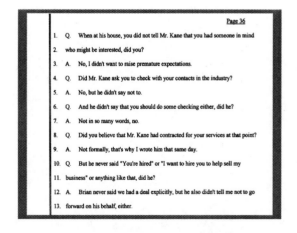

Quinlan p. 36 1–13 **Slide 54**

Easy Tech: Cases and Materials on Courtroom Technology
© The National Institute for Trial Advocacy

Quinlan video　　　　**Slide 55**

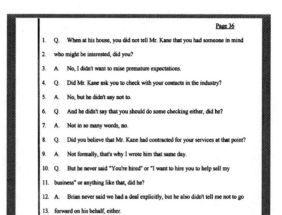

Quinlan Q & A reveal　**Slide 56**

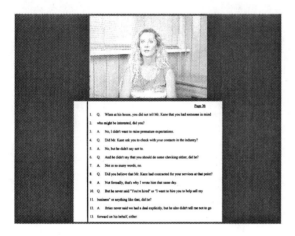

Quinlan video +　　　**Slide 57**

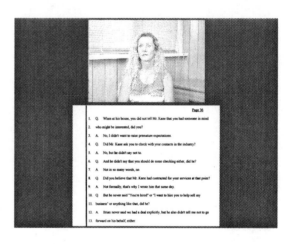

Quinlan video +　　　**Slide 58**

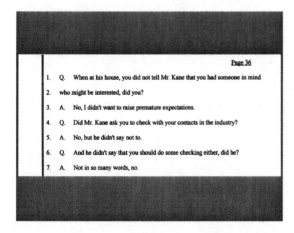

Quinlan p. 36 1–7　　**Slide 59**

Quinlan video　　　　**Slide 60**

Easy Tech: Cases and Materials on Courtroom Technology
© The National Institute for Trial Advocacy

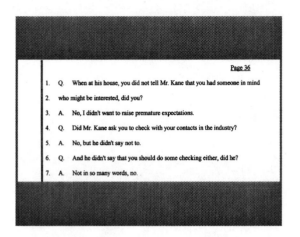

Quinlan Q & A reveal **Slide 61**

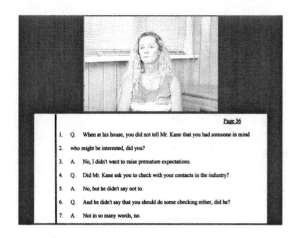

Quinlan video + **Slide 62**

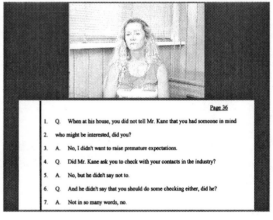

Quinlan video + **Slide 63**

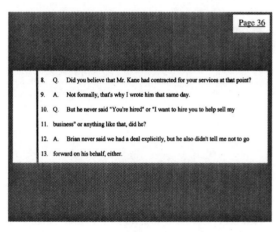

Quinlan p. 36 8–13 **Slide 64**

Quinlan video **Slide 65**

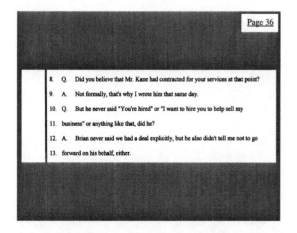

Quinlan Q & A reveal **Slide 66**

Easy Tech: Cases and Materials on Courtroom Technology
© The National Institute for Trial Advocacy

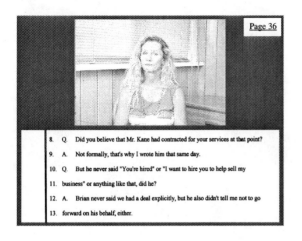

Quinlan video +   **Slide 67**

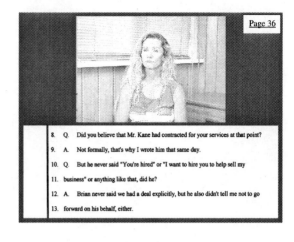

Quinlan video +   **Slide 68**

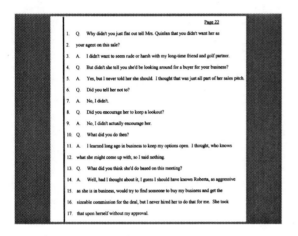

Kane p. 22 1–17   **Slide 69**

Kane video   **Slide 70**

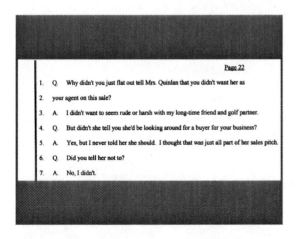

Kane p. 22 1–7   **Slide 71**

Kane video   **Slide 72**

Easy Tech: Cases and Materials on Courtroom Technology
© The National Institute for Trial Advocacy

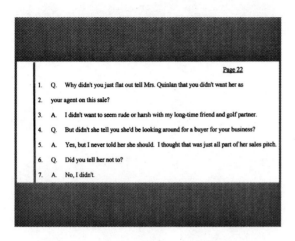

Kane Q & A reveal   **Slide 73**

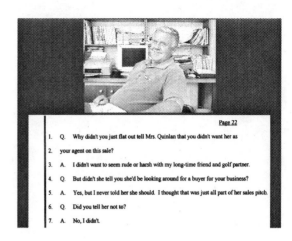

Kane video +   **Slide 74**

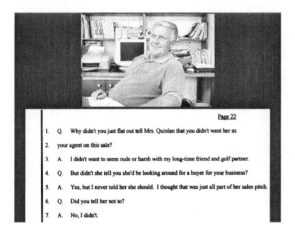

Kane video +   **Slide 75**

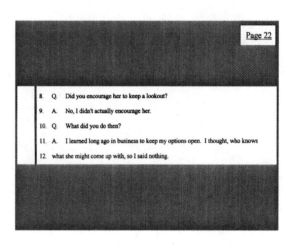

Kane p. 22 8–12   **Slide 76**

Kane video   **Slide 77**

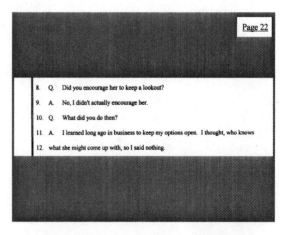

Kane Q & A reveal   **Slide 78**

Easy Tech: Cases and Materials on Courtroom Technology
© The National Institute for Trial Advocacy

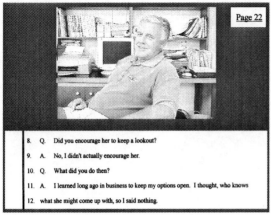

8. Q. Did you encourage her to keep a lookout?

9. A. No, I didn't actually encourage her.

10. Q. What did you do then?

11. A. I learned long ago in business to keep my options open. I thought, who knows

12. what she might come up with, so I said nothing.

Kane video +   **Slide 79**

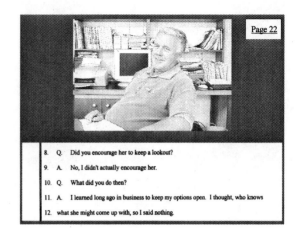

8. Q. Did you encourage her to keep a lookout?

9. A. No, I didn't actually encourage her.

10. Q. What did you do then?

11. A. I learned long ago in business to keep my options open. I thought, who knows

12. what she might come up with, so I said nothing.

Kane video +   **Slide 80**

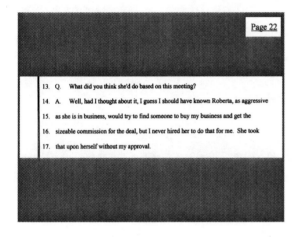

13. Q. What did you think she'd do based on this meeting?

14. A. Well, had I thought about it, I guess I should have known Roberta, as aggressive

15. as she is in business, would try to find someone to buy my business and get the

16. sizeable commission for the deal, but I never hired her to do that for me. She took

17. that upon herself without my approval.

Kane p. 22 13–17   **Slide 81**

Kane video   **Slide 82**

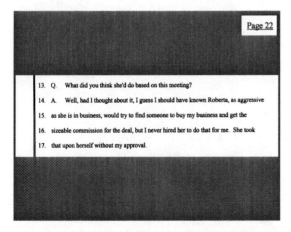

13. Q. What did you think she'd do based on this meeting?

14. A. Well, had I thought about it, I guess I should have known Roberta, as aggressive

15. as she is in business, would try to find someone to buy my business and get the

16. sizeable commission for the deal, but I never hired her to do that for me. She took

17. that upon herself without my approval.

Kane Q & A reveal   **Slide 83**

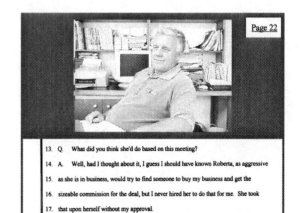

13. Q. What did you think she'd do based on this meeting?

14. A. Well, had I thought about it, I guess I should have known Roberta, as aggressive

15. as she is in business, would try to find someone to buy my business and get the

16. sizeable commission for the deal, but I never hired her to do that for me. She took

17. that upon herself without my approval.

Kane video +   **Slide 84**

Easy Tech: Cases and Materials on Courtroom Technology
© The National Institute for Trial Advocacy

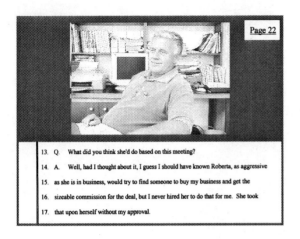

Kane video +   **Slide 85**

The Duck   **Slide 87**

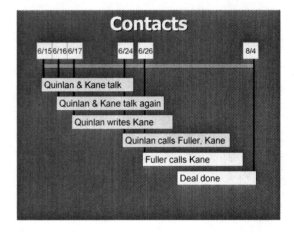

The Meeting   **Slide 86**

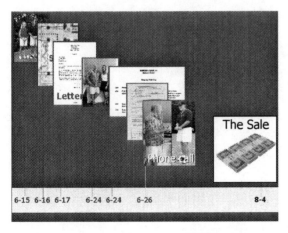

Time line   **Slide 89**

Contacts   **Slide 88**

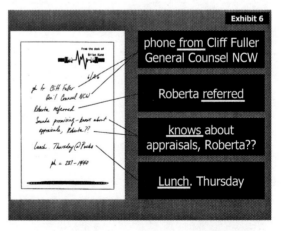

Exhibit 6   **Slide 90**

Seller owes   **Slide 91**

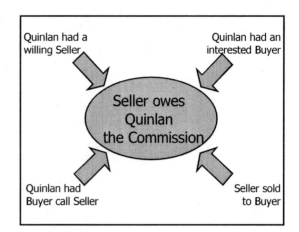

Seller owes   **Slide 92**

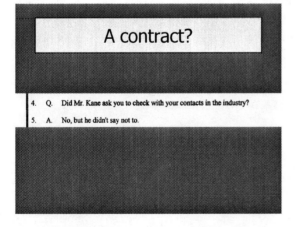

Quinlan must prove   **Slide 93**

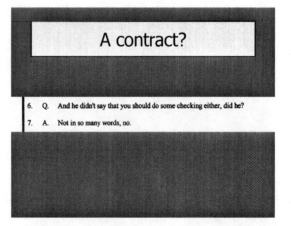

A contract?   **Slide 94**

A contract?

4.   Q.   Did Mr. Kane ask you to check with your contacts in the industry?

5.   A.   No, but he didn't say not to.

A contract?   **Slide 95**

A contract?

6.   Q.   And he didn't say that you should do some checking either, did he?

7.   A.   Not in so many words, no.

A contract?   **Slide 96**

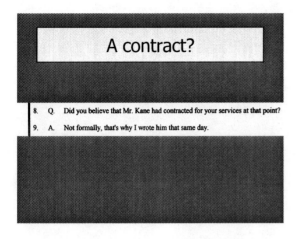

A contract?   **Slide 97**

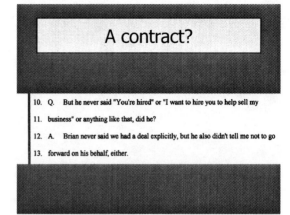

A contract?   **Slide 98**

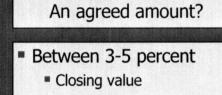

An agreed amount?   **Slide 99**

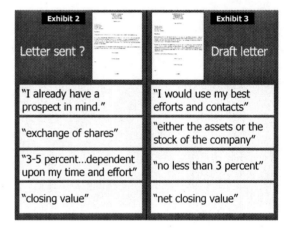

Exhibit 2 & 3   **Slide 100**

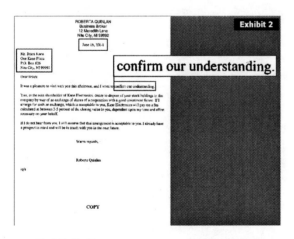

Exhibit 2   **Slide 101**

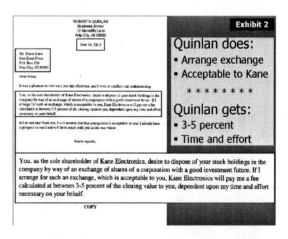

Exhibit 2   **Slide 102**

Easy Tech: Cases and Materials on Courtroom Technology
© The National Institute for Trial Advocacy

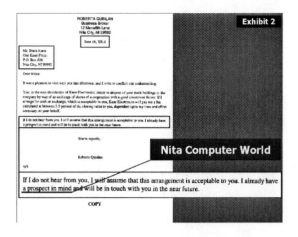

Exhibit 2   **Slide 103**

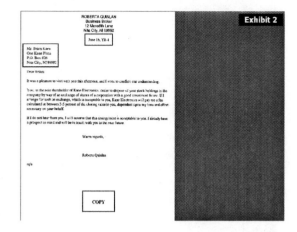

Exhibit 2   **Slide 104**

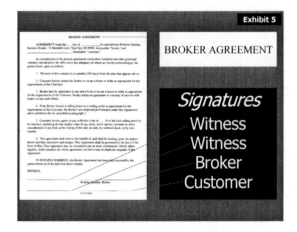

Exhibit 5   **Slide 105**

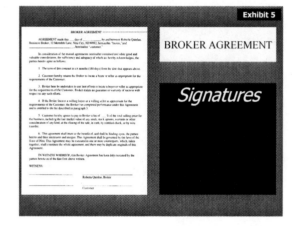

Exhibit 5   **Slide 106**

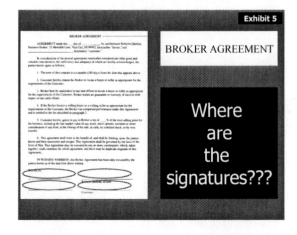

Exhibit 5   **Slide 107**

Blank slide   **Slide 108**

Easy Tech: Cases and Materials on Courtroom Technology
© The National Institute for Trial Advocacy

PROBLEM 1
(Exhibits: Quinlan letter)

For the Plaintiff, introduce the June 16, YR-1, letter from Quinlan to Kane (Exhibit 2) in evidence. When showing the proposed exhibit to the court, opposing counsel, and the witness for foundational purposes, utilize the electronic form of the exhibit. Assume the judge can prevent the jury from viewing the document until it is introduced in evidence.

For the Defendant, oppose the offer.

PROBLEM 2
(Exhibits: Form contract)

For the Defendant, introduce Quinlan's form contract (Exhibit 5) in evidence. When showing the proposed exhibit to the court, opposing counsel, and the witness for foundational purposes, utilize the electronic form of the exhibit. Assume the judge can prevent the jury from viewing the document until it is introduced in evidence.

For the Plaintiff, oppose the offer.

PROBLEM 3
(Exhibits: Photos)

For the Plaintiff, introduce the photos of Quinlan and Fuller (Exhibits 9 and 10) in evidence and make use of them in the direct examination of Quinlan utilizing the evidence camera as the display device.

For the Defendant, oppose the offer and use.

PROBLEM 4
(Exhibits: Photos)

For the Defendant, introduce the photos of Kane and Quinlan (Exhibits 7 and 8) in evidence and make use of them in the direct examination of Kane utilizing the evidence camera as the display device.

For the Plaintiff, oppose the offer and use.

PROBLEM 5
(Direct examination with illustrative aid: Diagram)

For the Plaintiff, examine Quinlan regarding the location of the June 16, YR-1 meeting between Quinlan and Kane using the diagram (Exhibit 11) as an illustrative aid.

Part A: Use the evidence camera and marker pen as your display device during the examination.

Part B: Use the computer and telestrator as your display device during the examination.

For the Defendant, oppose the offer and use.

PROBLEM 6
(Direct examination with illustrative aid: Diagram)

For the Defendant, examine Kane regarding the location of the meeting of June 16 between Kane and Quinlan utilizing the diagram (Exhibit 11) as an illustrative aid.

Part A: Use the evidence camera and marking pen as your display device during the examination.

Part B: Use the computer and telestrator as your display device during the examination.

For the Defendant, oppose the offer and use in Parts A and B.

PROBLEM 7
(Direct examination with exhibit: Quinlan letter)

For the Plaintiff, conduct the direct examination of Quinlan regarding her agreement with Kane utilizing Exhibit 2. For the purposes of this problem, assume that Exhibit 2 has been admitted in evidence.

Part A: Use the evidence camera and marking pen as your display device.

Part B: Use the computer and the telestrator as your display device.

Part C: Use the computer slide show with callouts and bullet points (PowerPoint slides #101–104, on the CD) as your display device.

For the Defendant, oppose the offer and use of the exhibits in Parts A, B, and C.

Easy Tech: Cases and Materials on Courtroom Technology
© The National Institute for Trial Advocacy

PROBLEM 8
(Cross-examination with exhibit: Form contract)

For the Defendant, conduct the cross-examination of Quinlan concerning her claim of an agreement with Kane utilizing her standard broker agreement (Exhibit 5) which was not used in this matter. For the purposes of this problem, assume that Exhibit 5 has been admitted in evidence.

Part A: Use the evidence camera and marking pen as your display device.

Part B: Use the computer and telestrator as your display device.

Part C: Use the computer slide show with callouts and bullet points (PowerPoint slides #105–106, on the CD) as your display device.

For the Plaintiff, oppose the offer and use of the exhibits in Parts A, B, and C.

PROBLEM 9
(Impeachment using transcript/video excerpt: Quinlan)

On direct examination the Plaintiff has testified to the following, "I told Brian that my fee would be as little as 3 percent depending on how involved I had to be in putting the deal together. I also told him that I already had a prospect in mind, and if that prospect came through, that I was sure the fee would be on the low end. He said, 'sounds good to me, let's get at it' or something like that. There was no question we had a deal; he was hot to move on the deal."

For the Defendant, conduct the impeachment of Quinlan.

Part A: Conduct the impeachment of Quinlan utilizing whatever portions you choose of the transcript of her testimony that appears in this volume.

Part B: Conduct the impeachment of Quinlan utilizing whatever portions you choose of her deposition testimony which appear in the PowerPoint slide show on your CD.

Part C: Conduct the impeachment of Quinlan utilizing whatever portions you choose of the videotape of her deposition testimony with the reveal of the written transcript appearing beneath it which appear in the PowerPoint slide show on your CD.

For the Plaintiff, oppose the impeachment and the use of exhibits in Parts A, B, and C.

Easy Tech: Cases and Materials on Courtroom Technology
© The National Institute for Trial Advocacy

PROBLEM 10
(Impeachment using transcript/video excerpt: Kane)

On direct examination the Defendant has testified to the following:

"I told Roberta I really wanted to do this deal myself. When she pressed on, saying she had potential buyers in mind that she wanted to contact, I politely told her to forget it. This was my deal, not hers."

For the Plaintiff, conduct the impeachment of Kane.

Part A: Conduct the impeachment of Kane utilizing whatever portions you choose of the transcript of his testimony that appears in this volume.

Part B: Conduct the impeachment of Kane utilizing whatever portions you choose of his deposition testimony which appear in the PowerPoint slide show on your CD.

Part C: Conduct the impeachment of Kane utilizing whatever portions you choose of the videotape of his deposition testimony with the reveal of the written transcript appearing beneath it which appear in the PowerPoint slide show on your CD.

For the Defendant, oppose the impeachment and the use of exhibits in Part A, B, and C.

PROBLEM 11
(Direct and cross-examination: Quinlan)

For the State, conduct the direct examination of Roberta Quinlan utilizing the exhibits and illustrative aids available in the file of your own choosing.

For the Defendant, conduct the cross-examination of Quinlan utilizing the exhibits and illustrative aids available in the file of your own choosing.

PROBLEM 12
(Direct and cross-examination: Kane)

For the State, conduct the direct examination of Brian Kane utilizing the exhibits and illustrative aids available in the file of your own choosing.

For the Defendant, conduct the cross-examination of Kane utilizing the exhibits and illustrative aids available in the file of your own choosing.

PROBLEM 13
(Direct and cross-examination: Fuller)

For the State, conduct the direct examination of Cliff Fuller utilizing the exhibits and illustrative aids available in the file of your own choosing.

For the Defendant, conduct the cross-examination of Fuller utilizing the exhibits and illustrative aids available in the file of your own choosing.

PROBLEM 14
(Direct and cross-examination: Edmonson)

For the State, conduct the direct examination of Margaret Edmonson utilizing the exhibits and illustrative aids available in the file of your own choosing.

For the Defendant, conduct the cross-examination of Edmonson utilizing the exhibits and illustrative aids available in the file of your own choosing.

PROBLEM 15
(Opening statement)

Prepare a ten-minute portion of the opening statement for your client in the case of *Quinlan v. Kane.* Assume the trial judge has ruled that you may utilize any evidentiary exhibit (in hard copy or in electronic form, displayed in the manner of your own choosing) in the case during the opening statement. Any illustrative aids, either from the file or of your own creation, must be shown to your opponent, who will have an opportunity to make objections for the judge's ruling. A brief hearing on the use of illustrative aids will be conducted. The hearing does not count toward the ten-minute portion of the opening statement assigned by the problem.

PROBLEM 16
(Closing argument)

Prepare a fifteen-minute portion of the closing argument for your client in the case of *Quinlan v. Kane.* In performing this exercise you may utilize any admissible evidentiary exhibit. In addition, you must use **at least** one illustrative aid from the file or of your own creation. The evidentiary exhibits and illustrative aids may be displayed in any form, utilizing the display device of your choosing. The choice and use of exhibits and illustrative aids will be one of the points of critique for this exercise.

Easy Tech: Cases and Materials on Courtroom Technology
© The National Institute for Trial Advocacy

State v. Lawrence
Criminal Case

State v. Lawrence
Contents

PART IV: State v. Lawrence[1]

Fact Summary

James Lawrence has been charged with assault and theft as a result of a purse-snatching incident on the evening of Friday, July 1, YR-1.[2] The victim was Gale Fitzgerald, a twenty-eight-year-old woman who works as a paralegal for a law firm in Nita City.

On Friday, July 1, YR-1, Fitzgerald was at the end of a long week preparing for trial and had worked late. She left the office at 9:15 p.m. and was on her way home from work. She got off the bus at the corner of 5th and Main at 9:45 p.m. and walked east on Main toward her apartment at 406 Main. At about the middle of the block on which her apartment building is located, she heard footsteps behind her and felt a sharp pull on her purse. She struggled briefly with her attacker. He threw her to the ground and ran off with the purse across the street and back towards 5th Street.

Fitzgerald reported the crime to the police on the evening it happened and gave a statement that evening to Officer James Wright. She visited the police station at Wright's request on July 3, YR-1, and looked at mug books, which included a photo of Lawrence taken two years before, but was unable to identify anyone. A report of that meeting was prepared by Officer Wright.

On July 15, YR-1, Lawrence was arrested in an attempt to snatch the purse of an off-duty police officer, Sonia Henderson. A current mug shot was duly made, and Officer Wright called Fitzgerald to come to the station and look at the current mug shot of Lawrence together with four photos of other white males. Fitzgerald identified Lawrence. A videotape was made of the procedure and a transcript was prepared.

When arrested for the Henderson purse snatching, Lawrence was given his Miranda warning and chose to waive his right to remain silent and gave a statement. That statement was videotaped and transcribed. He told police that he was on a movie date on Friday, July 1, YR-1. When the movie was over, he took his date to her house and kissed her goodnight. He denied any involvement in the Fitzgerald purse snatching. When contacted by Officer Wright, Chelsea Williams said that she was at a movie with Lawrence that evening, and he took her home, but she could not remember exactly when she reached home.

The defense brought a successful motion in limine with respect to Lawrence's attempt to snatch the purse of the police officer. Lawrence's previous arrest for assault on April 1, YR-3, resulted in a guilty plea to a misdemeanor for which he received a six-month suspended sentence with ten days to serve.

---

1. The *State v. Lawrence* case is adapted from *State v. Lawrence Case File* by William Burnham and James H. Seckinger (NITA, 1992).

2. NITA uses a convention for dates as follows: YR-0 (this year), YR-1 (last year), YR-2 (two years ago) and so on. Students should use the actual year in working on the exercises.

JURY INSTRUCTIONS

1. The Court will now instruct you about the law that governs this case. By your oath, you agreed to accept and follow these instructions and to apply them to the facts you find from the evidence. Any verdict in this case must be the unanimous decision of all jurors.

2. The State of Nita claims that the Defendant, James Lawrence, committed the offenses of (a) Assault in the Third Degree, and (b) Theft in the Second Degree. By his "Not Guilty" plea, the defendant denied each of those charges. You should consider each of the charges separately, and your verdict for either charge should not influence your verdict as to the other charge.

3. The State of Nita has the burden of proving each of those charges beyond a reasonable doubt. A reasonable doubt is a doubt based on reason and common sense which remains after a full, fair, and rational consideration of all the evidence. It is not a vague, speculative, or imaginary doubt. Proof beyond a reasonable doubt is proof upon which reasonable persons would rely and act for matters of great importance to themselves.

4. To prove the charge of Assault in the Third Degree, the State of Nita must prove beyond a reasonable doubt:

   a. On or about July 1, YR-1, in the State and County of Nita;

   b. The Defendant caused bodily harm to Gale Fitzgerald. "Bodily harm" is any physical injury, regardless of its gravity or duration; and

   c. In causing that harm, the Defendant acted intentionally, knowingly, or recklessly.
       To do an act "intentionally" is to do it purposely and not accidentally. A person acts "knowingly," regardless of his purpose, when he is aware that his conduct will probably cause a certain result. A person acts "recklessly" if he acts carelessly or negligently with a conscious disregard for probable consequences.

5. To prove the charge of Theft in the Second Degree, the State of Nita must prove beyond a reasonable doubt:

   a. On or about July 1, YR-1, in the State and County of Nita;

   b. The Defendant obtained or exerted unauthorized control over Gale Fitzgerald's property;

   c. He obtained Gale Fitzgerald's property from Gale Fitzgerald's personal possession; and

   d. He acted with the intent or purpose of depriving her of that property.

Easy Tech: Cases and Materials on Courtroom Technology
© The National Institute for Trial Advocacy

STATE OF NITA   :
                                       :
    Plaintiff   :   CRIMINAL CASE NO. 6725
vs.   :
                                       :   <u>VERDICT FORM</u>
JAMES LAWRENCE   :
                                       :
    Defendant   :

We, the jury, unanimously find:

MARK AN "X" FOR THE CORRECT VERDICT ON EACH CHARGE SEPARATELY

1. For the charge of Assault in the Third Degree, we find

    _____   The defendant, James Lawrence, Guilty.

    _____   The defendant, James Lawrence, Not Guilty.

2. For the charge of Theft in the Second Degree, we find

    _____   The defendant, James Lawrence, Guilty.

    _____   The defendant, James Lawrence, Not Guilty.

_____
Foreperson

EXHIBIT 1

NITA CITY POLICE DEPARTMENT
Nita City, Nita

INVESTIGATIVE REPORT

1. Complaining Witness Gale Fitzgerald	2. Address 406 Main Street, Nita City, NI
3. Phone 449-5237 (home) 889-9000 (work)	4. Complained of Offense Theft, Assault (purse snatching)
5. Date July 1, YR-1	6. Place 400 block of Main Street Nita City

7. Narrative

Complaining witness interviewed at her apartment at above address. States that upon exiting bus at 5th and Main and walking towards her apartment, was grabbed from behind by unknown assailant. Struggle ensues. Assailant stole purse belonging to complaining witness containing personal articles, including wallet and $400 in cash. Witness agrees to come to station on 7/3 on lunch break to attempt mug shot ID and to sign statement (See attached statement).

7/3/YR-1
Complaining witness comes to station at 1300 hours. Reviews and signs statement given two nights previous. Shown several mug books of known purse snatchers. Not able to make positive ID. Purse containing wallet with ID for Gale Fitzgerald found in mailbox at 814 Main Street. Purse identified by Ms. Fitzgerald as hers. States that everything but money still in the purse. Reviews and signs supplemental statement (See attached supplemental statement).

7/15/YR-1
Interview with James Lawrence at city jail. Lawrence being held on attempted theft and assault charges for trying to steal by force the purse of off-duty police officer, Sonia Henderson. Advise suspect of investigation of July 1 incident and other purse snatchings. Advised of his Miranda rights. Waived. (See signed waiver form attached.) Suspect says he has an alibi for July 1 incident. Went to movies with Chelsea Williams, 1013 Elm Street, Nita City. Gives signed statement (attached).

10. Investigating Officer - Name and Signature

James Wright

James Wright, Badge #007

Easy Tech: Cases and Materials on Courtroom Technology
© The National Institute for Trial Advocacy

NITA CITY POLICE DEPARTMENT
Nita City, Nita

INVESTIGATIVE REPORT

1. Complaining Witness Gale Fitzgerald	2. Address 406 Main Street, Nita City, NI
3. Phone 449-5237 (home) 889-9000 (work)	4. Complained of Offense Theft, Assault (purse snatching)
5. Date July 1, YR-1	6. Place 400 block of Main Street Nita City

7. Narrative

7/16/YR-1

Complaining witness called to station. Suspect who meets description given by Ms. Fitzgerald arrested on 7/15 in attempt to snatch purse of off-duty police officer. Ms. Fitzgerald shown array of photos including recent photo of suspect, James Lawrence. Positive ID made. Obtain purse from Ms. Fitzgerald as evidence in the case against Lawrence. This officer notes that photograph of suspect was among those included in mug books complaining witness viewed on 7/3/YR-1.

7/18/YR-1

Contact alibi witness, Chelsea Williams, at job. Arrange for interview at police station on 7/19 before she goes to work.

7/19/YR-1

Meet with Chelsea Williams at 0900. Agrees to give signed statement (See signed statement attached.) This officer notes that Ms. Williams lives no more than a ten minute walk from the crime scene in this case.

10. Investigating Officer - Name and Signature

James Wright

James Wright, Badge #007

EXHIBIT 2

STATEMENT OF GALE FITZGERALD
JULY 3, YR-1

My name is Gale Fitzgerald. I am twenty-eight years old. I am single and live in an apartment at 406 Main Street in Nita City. I work for Harry Loomis, a personal injury lawyer, as a secretary and paralegal. His offices are in the Public Ledger Building in downtown Nita City.

On July 1, YR-1, I worked late. Harry was in the middle of a trial and we had been at the office until at least 9:00 p.m. every night for the week before July 1st. I left the office at 9:15 p.m. and got lucky and caught a bus right away outside the building. The bus, which travels up 5th Street, let me off at the bus stop at the corner of 5th and Main Streets at about 9:45 p.m. I got off the bus and started to walk east on the sidewalk toward my apartment. There are streetlights on the corners of the intersection and some small lights on the houses on that block. I would say that the visibility was fairly good given that it was nighttime.

As I walked towards my apartment, I completed the 500 block and entered the block my apartment is on. As I got to a fire hydrant at about the middle of the block, I heard fast footsteps behind me. Before I could turn around I felt a sharp pull on my purse, which I was carrying on my right shoulder. The tug on the purse turned me around and I was facing my attacker. I know it was stupid, but I struggled with him. I had taken $400 out of the ATM in our building just before I left for the night and didn't want to lose it. I also had in my purse a letter I received at the office from a good friend that I hadn't yet had a chance to read.

We struggled over the purse for what seemed like a long time, but I guess was less than 15 seconds, until he threw me to the ground. Somehow the strap broke on my purse and my attacker ran off with my purse across the street and in the direction that he came from, towards 5th Street. My attacker was a white man, approximately 5'8" to 5'10" in height, 160–175 pounds, with dark hair (dark brown or black), wearing dark pants, a white tank-top shirt, and running shoes.

As soon as I got into my apartment I called the police. Officer Wright came to my apartment soon afterwards, where I am now giving this statement. That's all I can remember. I am very upset by this. I've never been attacked before.

Signed: _Gale Fitzgerald_
Gale Fitzgerald
July 3, YR-1

Easy Tech: Cases and Materials on Courtroom Technology
© The National Institute for Trial Advocacy

EXHIBIT 3

SUPPLEMENTAL STATEMENT OF GALE FITZGERALD
JULY 3, YR-1

I have come to the police station today at the request of Officer Jim Wright. Officer Wright returned my purse to me, which he told me was recovered from a mailbox in the 800 block of Main Street.

The purse has a torn shoulder strap. All of my personal belongings and my wallet with all my identification are still in it. All of my money, including the money I took out of the ATM before going home on the day of the mugging, is gone.

I have been shown several books of mug shot photographs and have not been able to identify my attacker among them.

Signed: _Gale Fitzgerald_
Gale Fitzgerald
July 3, YR-1

EXHIBIT 4

NITA CITY POLICE DEPARTMENT
Nita City, Nita

WAIVER OF RIGHTS

1. Complaining Witness Sonia Henderson	2. Address Nita City Police Department
3. Phone 889-9000 (work)	4. Complained of Offense Theft, Assault (purse snatching)
5. Date July 15, YR-1	6. Place 6th & Davenport St. Nita City

I am ___James Lawrence___ . I have been given my rights. I understand that I do not have to make any statement whatsoever, that I have a right to remain silent, that I have a right to have a lawyer present, and that anything I say should I give a statement could be used against me in a court of law. Knowing those rights, I am freely and voluntarily agreeing to talk with an officer of the Nita City Police Department and waive those rights with regard to the matter described on the top of this form.

James Lawrence
NAME (signed)

James Wright
WITNESS NAME (signed)

___July 15, YR-1___
DATE

EXHIBIT 5

STATEMENT OF JAMES LAWRENCE

Taken by Officer James Wright

Wright: It's July 15, I'm Officer James Wright of the Nita City Police Department. It's 10:30 p.m. The suspect, Mr. Lawrence, has chosen to give a statement. We are recording this statement in an interview room at the Nita City Police Department by use of videotape. The proceedings will be transcribed for Mr. Lawrence's signature. All right then, let's begin.

Wright: What is your name and address?

Lawrence: James Lawrence, 523 Maple Street, Nita City.

Q.   You understand that you are under arrest for the attempted robbery of Sonia Henderson, do you not?

A.   Yes.

Q.   And you've been given your Miranda rights and are voluntarily choosing to speak with me, is that correct?

A.   Yes.

Q.   Just to be clear sir, I am showing you a document that's titled "Waiver of Rights," and it has a signature on it. Is that your signature?

A.   Yes.

Q.   What is your height and weight?

A.   I'm just over six feet tall and 175 pounds.

Q.   I want to ask you about another assault and purse snatching that happened in the recent past.

A.   I've never done this before, I don't know anything about any purse snatches.

Q.   Let me ask you this sir, where were you on the evening of July 1st at approximately 9:30 to 10:00 p.m.?

A.   Was that a Friday?

Q.   Yes, it was.

A.   Let's see. Friday a couple weeks ago. I was with my girlfriend, Chelsea Williams. We went over to get something to eat after her work and then down to the movies. We saw *To Kill a Mockingbird* at the Varsity Theater near her apartment. Then I walked her home. I stayed with Chelsea until sometime between 9:30 and 10:00. Then I walked home.

Q.   Do you ever use public transportation to get from Chelsea's apartment to home?

A.   Yeah, if the weather's really bad, or if I'm in a hurry. I'll take the number 9 bus which goes down Elm to 5th, and then goes down 5th to where I get off at Maple, which is just a half block from my apartment.

Q.   How did you walk home on July 1st?

A.   I always go the same way. She lives down 10th and Elm. I walk over to 8th Avenue, down 8th to Maple, and then over to my apartment at 523 Maple. I like to walk down 8th Avenue because there are some interesting stores and I like to window shop. I can't really afford the stuff in those shops, but it's nice to look.

Q.   Have you ever been to a bar near 8th and Main called Dorothy's?

A.   I'm not a regular or anything. It's pretty expensive but I've been in there. I don't drink much, maybe a beer or two, but that's it. Especially at those prices.

Q.   Were you at Dorothy's on the evening of July 1st of this year?

A.   I might have been but I don't think so. I was really short of money a couple of weeks ago. I had just paid my rent and my customers, I do lawns and yard clean-up for people, had been slow in paying. I couldn't even afford to pay for Chelsea's meal at some fast-food place that night, so I doubt if I stopped into Dorothy's.

Q.   Do you know a woman named Gale Fitzgerald?

A.   No, never heard of her.

Q.   Have you ever been to her neighborhood, at 4th and Main?

A.   I might have. It's only a couple blocks from my apartment, but I have no reason to go to that block.

Q.   Do you know any reason why Ms. Fitzgerald would identify you as the man who stole her purse and shoved her to the ground on July 1st of this year at about 9:45 p.m.?

Easy Tech: Cases and Materials on Courtroom Technology
© The National Institute for Trial Advocacy

A.   No. If she said so she must be mistaken, and it's dark at 9:45 at night and there are lots of trees in that neighborhood. Just houses, no stores. There aren't many street lights either.

Q.   Come on Jim. You needed the money, you saw this poor woman. You ripped her off just like Officer Henderson.

A.   I don't have to take this. That's all a bunch of bullshit. I want to see my lawyer.

Q.   It'll go easier on you if you just confess. Let's clear this up today. There's no need to drag it out. It really will . . .

A.   That's it. I want to see a lawyer now. You said I could have one if I wanted. Well I want one now.

Q.   OK. Your loss pal. This ends the statement of James Lawrence on July 15. Off record.

I have read the above three-page transcript and it is a true and accurate transcription of my statement to Officer James Wright given on July 15, YR-1.

James Lawrence
James Lawrence

Witness: _James Wright_
James Wright

EXHIBIT 6

Transcript — Gale Fitzgerald — 7/16/YR-1

Officer Wright:	The time is 5:18 p.m., the date July 16. We are in the Nita City Police Department conference room with Ms. Gale Fitzgerald. Ms. Fitzgerald, we're videotaping this session with your knowledge and permission, is that correct?
Ms. Fitzgerald:	Yes, that's true.
Officer Wright:	We've again asked you to come to the station to help us in our investigation of the mugging that took place on July 1st in which you were the victim. We have several photographs we'd like to show you. Please tell us if any of these five photos is of the man who attacked you and took your purse.
Ms. Fitzgerald:	Why yes, that's him, number 4. Oh yes, how did you know? What's his name. Has he done this before to others?
Officer Wright:	I can't tell you ma'am any details about our investigation. Are you certain this is the man who attacked you on July 1st?
Ms. Fitzgerald:	Well, I wouldn't put my life on it, it was dark you know, but I definitely recognize the tattoo on his right arm. His arm was right next to me. The face, there was barely enough light for me to see his face, and it was only for a few seconds. This looks like the guy. No, I'm sure this is the guy. It must be.
Officer Wright:	Thank you very much, Ms. Fitzgerald. We'll be letting you know when you're needed for trial. Off record.

EXHIBIT 7

SUPPLEMENTAL STATEMENT OF GALE FITZGERALD
JULY 16, YR-1

I have come to the Nita City police station today at the request of Officer Jim Wright for the purpose of participating further in the investigation of the attack on me on July 1, YR-1.

I have been shown a series of five photographs. Photograph #4 is a photograph of an individual who I can positively identify as my attacker. I had never seen this man before July 1st when he attacked me. I am informed that the name of my attacker is James Lawrence.

At Officer Wright's request, I am returning my purse, which I haven't yet had the time to repair, to be kept as evidence in the case.

Signed: _____
Gale Fitzgerald
October 16, YR-1

EXHIBIT 8

STATEMENT OF CHELSEA WILLIAMS
JULY 19, YR-1

I have come to the police station today at the request of Officer Jim Wright. I am nineteen years old and live with two girlfriends in an apartment at 1013 Elm Street near the community college. I am a graduate of Nita High School. I currently work during the day as a clerk at the Sunglass Hut at the Nita Mall and go to night school at Nita Community College studying cosmetology.

I have known James Lawrence since high school. He was two years ahead of my class, but I remember him from then as a cool guy, always hanging out with the in crowd. He dropped out of school. I heard he left home and moved into an apartment with a bunch of guys not far from downtown. About two months ago he came by the Sunglass Hut and struck up a conversation with me. I was surprised because he had never given me the time of day back in high school. I couldn't talk long because I was at work, but he asked me to meet him after I got off to talk some more, which I did. We hit it off pretty good. He told me he lived with a couple of other guys from high school. I have been to the apartment. It is somewhere near 5th or 6th Avenue on Maple Street. We don't go there much, it's always such a mess. He also told me he had his own business doing yardwork and cleanup. We have been dating once or twice a week ever since. He is a good guy, no long hair or weird clothes. About two weeks ago he cut his hair really short, almost shaved. I didn't like it at first, but now that it has grown out a bit it looks pretty cool.

I know you want to talk with me because he's in some kind of trouble. He called me early yesterday morning from the jail telling me I might be getting a call from the police. He asked me questions about a date we had a few weeks ago when we went to the movies. I remembered the date and the movie, *To Kill A Mockingbird*, with Gregory Peck. It was playing at the Varsity Theater downtown, which specializes in old classic movies. When he asked me what night we saw that movie, I really couldn't recall either the day of the week or the actual date. After talking with Jim a little more, I finally realized it must have been a Friday, which would have made it the first of the month. My cosmetology classes are on Monday, Tuesday, and Wednesday nights, so I know it couldn't have been one of those nights. The Varsity usually only keeps movies for a week at a time before changing, and I do remember it was right around the beginning of the month when we saw the movie.

Whatever night it was, Jim met me when I got off from work at 5:00 and we walked over to Burger Queen to grab a bite, Dutch treat of course. Jim doesn't make a lot of money and even though it upsets him, I insist on paying my way. I remember that night he had just paid his rent. The movie started around 7:00. We got back to my apartment no later than 9:15 or 9:30. I remember I was feeling real tired, so Jim didn't stay long, maybe ten or fifteen minutes. I don't remember exactly what he was wearing, but he usually wears jeans, those air sneakers he loves so much, a tee shirt or tank top, and a light jacket, kind of dark in color.

Signed: _Chelsea Williams_

Chelsea Williams
July 19, YR-1

EXHIBIT 9

W — Williams Apartment
H — Henderson Assault by Lawrence
B — Dorothy's Bar--Mailbox Where Purse Found
L — Lawrence Apartment
X — Fitzgerald Assault
F — Fitzgerald Apartment

Easy Tech: Cases and Materials on Courtroom Technology
© The National Institute for Trial Advocacy

EXHIBIT 10

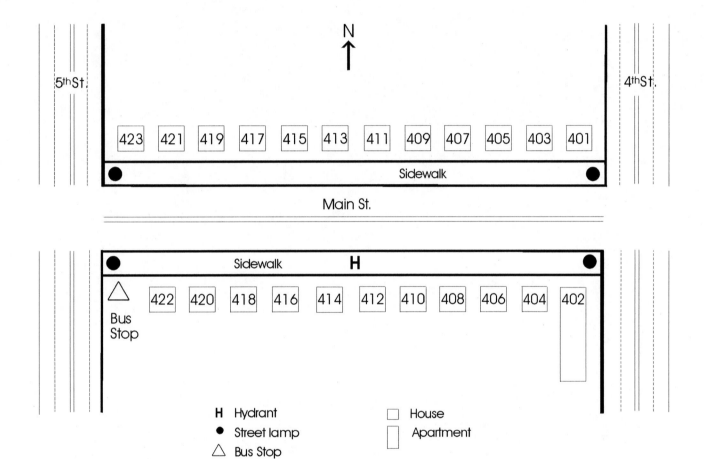

EXHIBIT 11

EXHIBIT 12

13A

13B

13C

13D

EXHIBIT 14

PHOTO ARRAY SHOWN TO VICTIM

7/1
theft/assault
Off. Wright

DEFENSE VERSION OF PHOTO ARRAY

7/1
theft/assault
Off. Wright

-175-
Easy Tech: Cases and Materials on Courtroom Technology
© The National Institute for Trial Advocacy

EXHIBIT 15

EXHIBIT 16

Easy Tech: Cases and Materials on Courtroom Technology
© The National Institute for Trial Advocacy

EXHIBIT 17

EXHIBIT 18

Easy Tech: Cases and Materials on Courtroom Technology
© The National Institute for Trial Advocacy

EXHIBIT 19

EXHIBIT 20

EXHIBIT 21

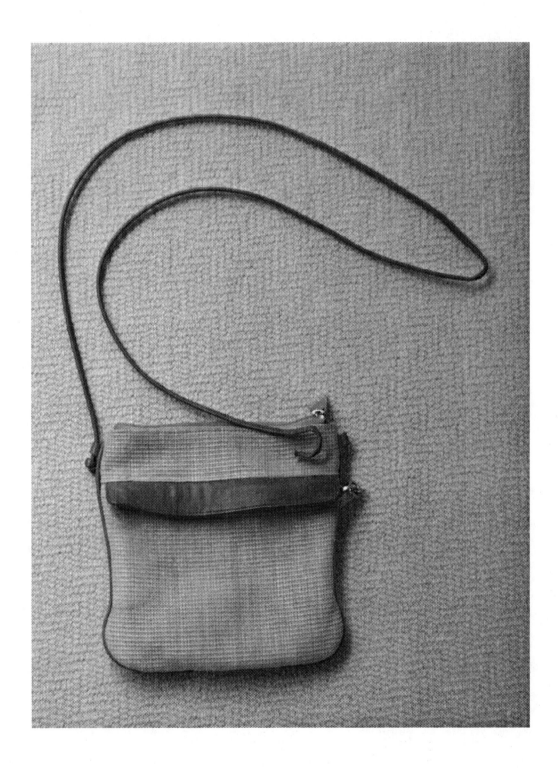

Easy Tech: Cases and Materials on Courtroom Technology
© The National Institute for Trial Advocacy

EXHIBIT 22

JULY YR-1

SUNDAY	MONDAY	TUESDAY	WEDNESDAY	THURSDAY	FRIDAY	SATURDAY
					1	2
3	4	5	6	7	8	9
10	11	12	13	14	15	16
17	18	19	20	21	22	23
24	25	26	27	28	29	30
31						

Easy Tech: Cases and Materials on Courtroom Technology
© The National Institute for Trial Advocacy

Blank Slide   **Slide 1**

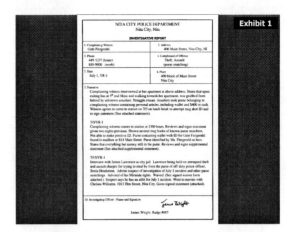

Exhibit 1, p. 1   **Slide 2**

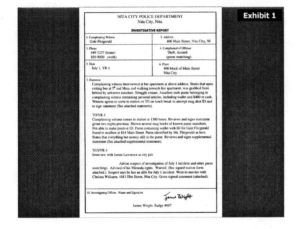

Exhibit 1, p. 1   **Slide 3**

Exhibit 1, p. 2   **Slide 4**

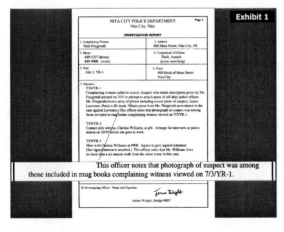

Exhibit 1   **Slide 5**

Exhibit 1   **Slide 6**

Easy Tech: Cases and Materials on Courtroom Technology

© The National Institute for Trial Advocacy

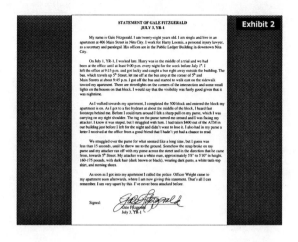

Exhibit 2   **Slide 7**

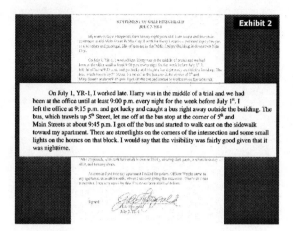

Exhibit 2   **Slide 8**

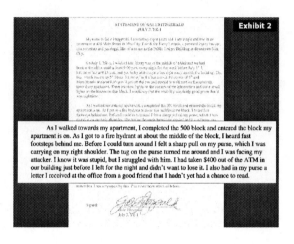

Exhibit 2   **Slide 9**

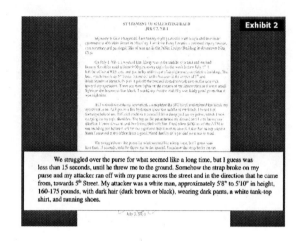

Exhibit 2   **Slide 10**

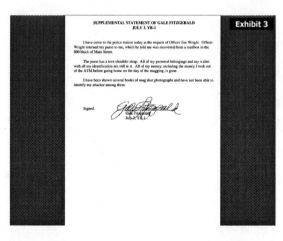

Exhibit 3   **Slide 11**

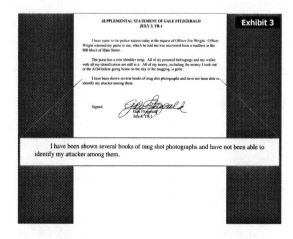

Exhibit 3   **Slide 12**

Easy Tech: Cases and Materials on Courtroom Technology
© The National Institute for Trial Advocacy

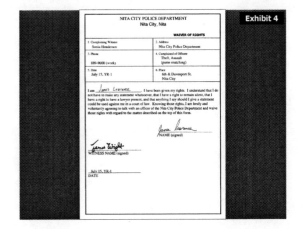

Exhibit 4   **Slide 13**

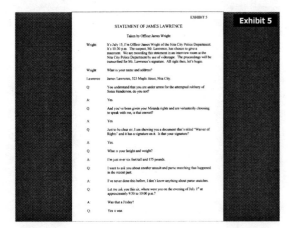

Exhibit 5, p. 1   **Slide 14**

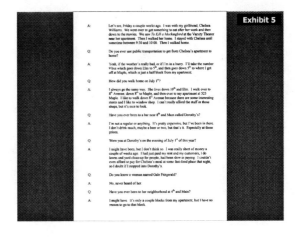

Exhibit 5, p. 2   **Slide 15**

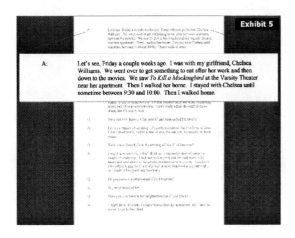

Exhibit 5, p. 2   **Slide 16**

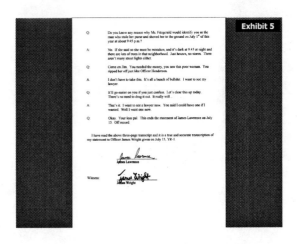

Exhibit 5, p. 3   **Slide 17**

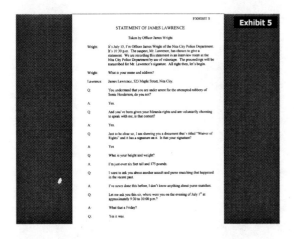

Exhibit 5   **Slide 18**

-191-

Easy Tech: Cases and Materials on Courtroom Technology
© The National Institute for Trial Advocacy

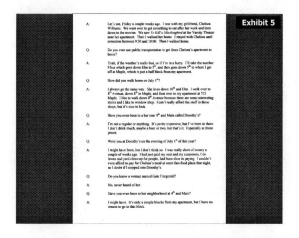

Exhibit 5   **Slide 19**

Exhibit 5   **Slide 20**

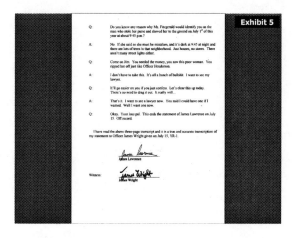

Exhibit 5   **Slide 21**

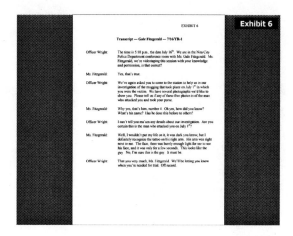

Exhibit 6   **Slide 22**

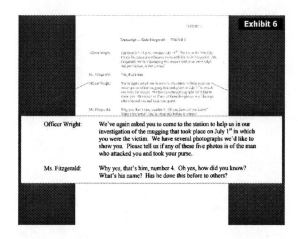

Exhibit 6   **Slide 23**

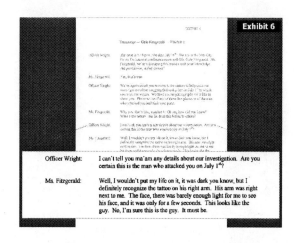

Exhibit 6   **Slide 24**

Easy Tech: Cases and Materials on Courtroom Technology
© The National Institute for Trial Advocacy

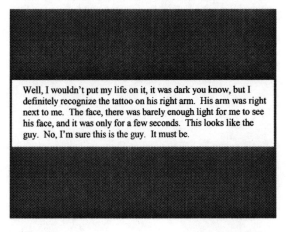

Exhibit 6   **Slide 25**

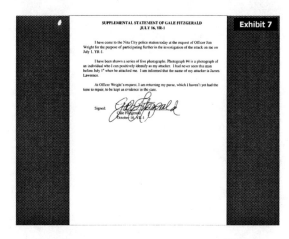

Exhibit 7   **Slide 26**

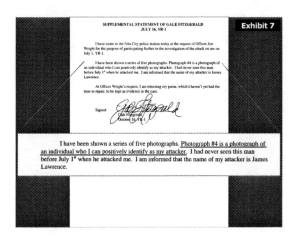

Exhibit 7   **Slide 27**

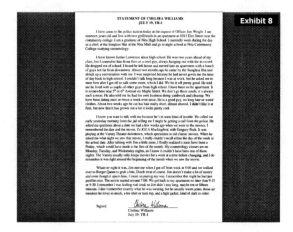

Exhibit 8   **Slide 28**

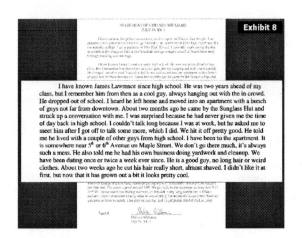

Exhibit 8   **Slide 29**

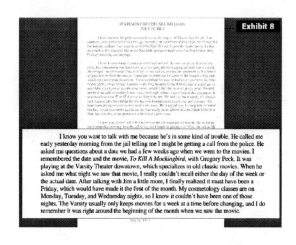

Exhibit 8   **Slide 30**

Easy Tech: Cases and Materials on Courtroom Technology
© The National Institute for Trial Advocacy

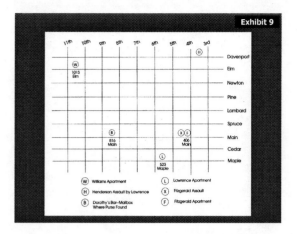

Exhibit 9   **Slide 31**

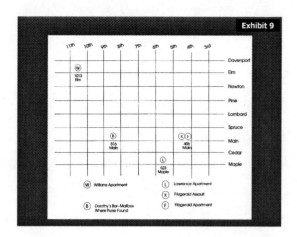

Exhibit 9   **Slide 32**

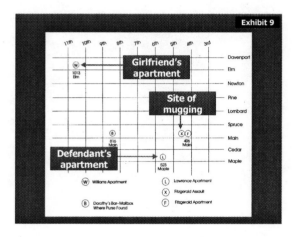

Exhibit 9   **Slide 33**

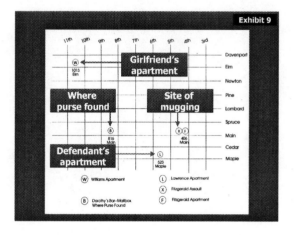

Exhibit 9   **Slide 34**

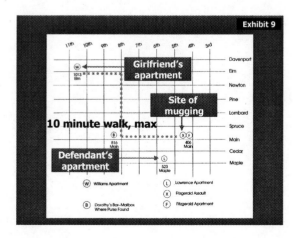

Exhibit 9   **Slide 35**

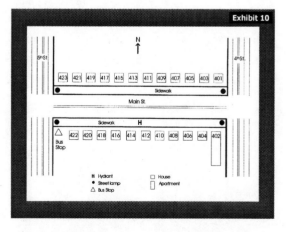

Exhibit 10   **Slide 36**

Easy Tech: Cases and Materials on Courtroom Technology
© The National Institute for Trial Advocacy

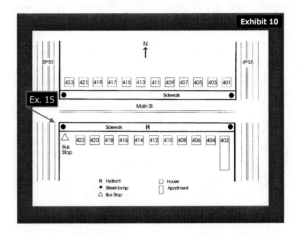

Exhibit 10   **Slide 37**

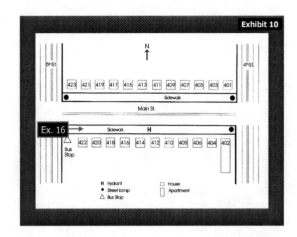

Exhibit 10   **Slide 38**

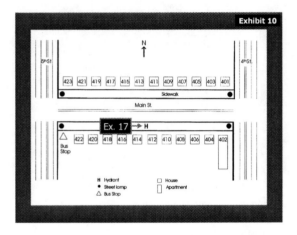

Exhibit 10   **Slide 39**

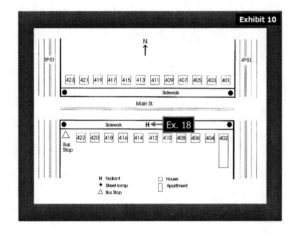

Exhibit 10   **Slide 40**

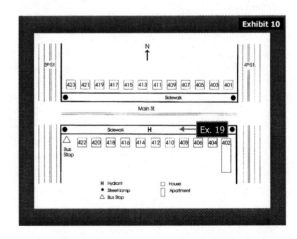

Exhibit 10   **Slide 41**

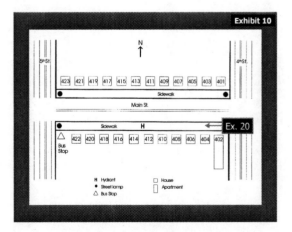

Exhibit 10   **Slide 42**

Easy Tech: Cases and Materials on Courtroom Technology
© The National Institute for Trial Advocacy

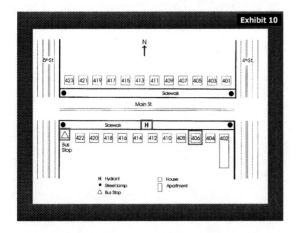

Exhibit 10   **Slide 43**

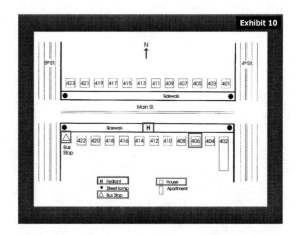

Exhibit 10   **Slide 44**

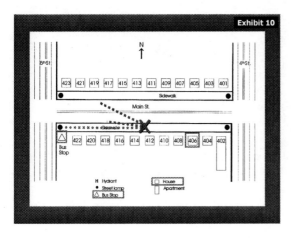

Exhibit 10   **Slide 45**

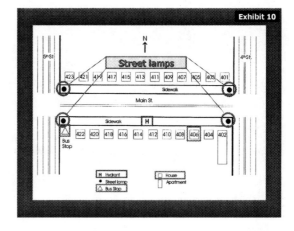

Exhibit 10   **Slide 46**

Exhibit 11   **Slide 47**

Exhibit 12   **Slide 48**

Easy Tech: Cases and Materials on Courtroom Technology
© The National Institute for Trial Advocacy

Exhibit 13a   **Slide 49**

Exhibit 13b   **Slide 50**

Exhibit 13c   **Slide 51**

Exhibit 13d   **Slide 52**

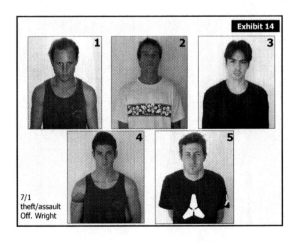

Exhibit 14   **Slide 53**

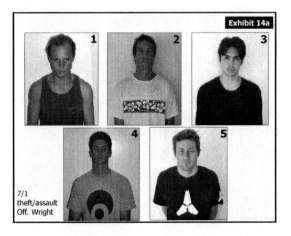

Exhibit 14a   **Slide 54**

Easy Tech: Cases and Materials on Courtroom Technology
© The National Institute for Trial Advocacy

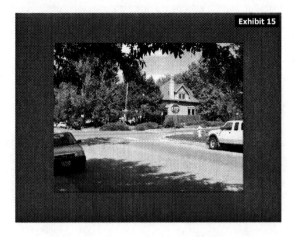

Exhibit 15   **Slide 55**

Exhibit 16   **Slide 56**

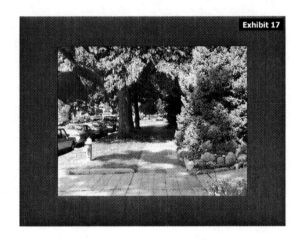

Exhibit 17   **Slide 57**

Exhibit 18   **Slide 58**

Exhibit 19   **Slide 59**

Exhibit 20   **Slide 60**

Easy Tech: Cases and Materials on Courtroom Technology
© The National Institute for Trial Advocacy

Exhibit 21   **Slide 61**

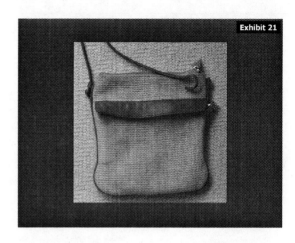

Exhibit 21   **Slide 62**

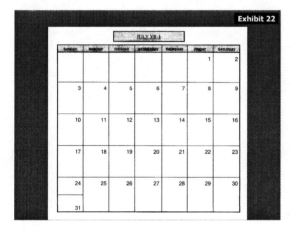

Exhibit 22   **Slide 63**

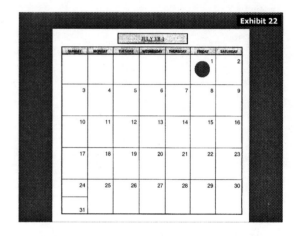

Exhibit 22   **Slide 64**

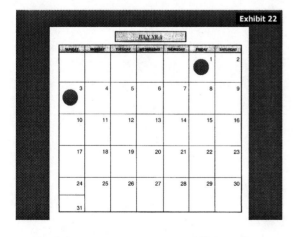

Exhibit 22   **Slide 65**

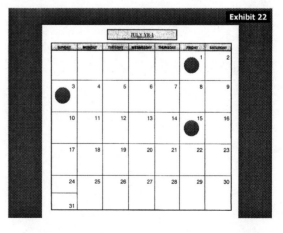

Exhibit 22   **Slide 66**

Easy Tech: Cases and Materials on Courtroom Technology
© The National Institute for Trial Advocacy

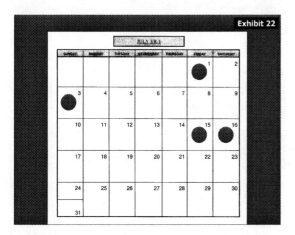

Exhibit 22   **Slide 67**

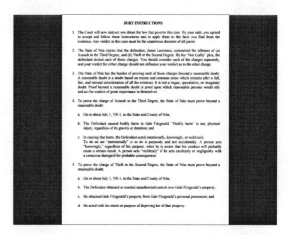

Jury Instructions   **Slide 68**

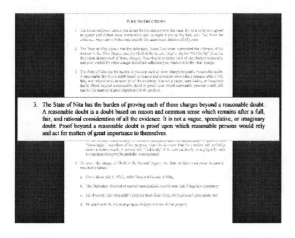

Jury Instruction 3   **Slide 69**

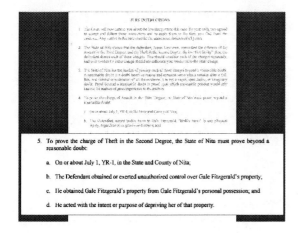

Jury Instruction 5   **Slide 71**

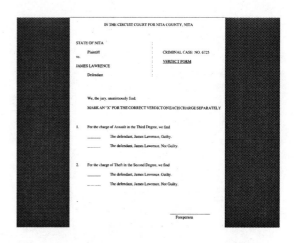

Verdict Form   **Slide 72**

Easy Tech: Cases and Materials on Courtroom Technology
© The National Institute for Trial Advocacy

Lawrence video   **Slide 73**

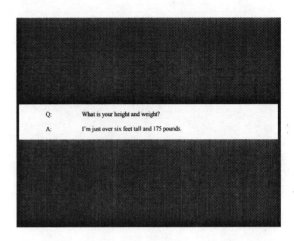

Height/weight   **Slide 74**

Lawrence video   **Slide 75**

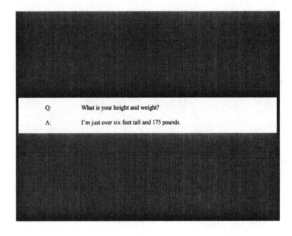

Lawrence reveal   **Slide 76**

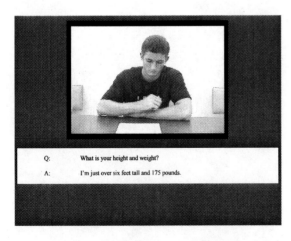

Lawrence video +   **Slide 77**

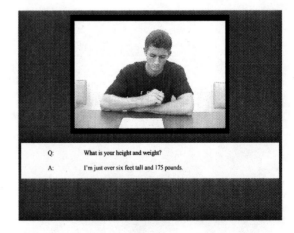

Lawrence video +   **Slide 78**

Easy Tech: Cases and Materials on Courtroom Technology
© The National Institute for Trial Advocacy

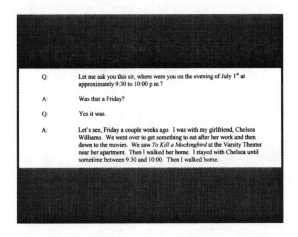

Let me ask   **Slide 79**

Video Let me   **Slide 80**

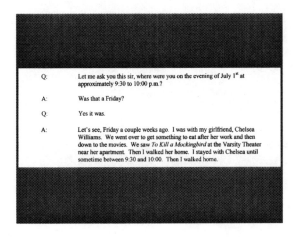

Let me reveal   **Slide 81**

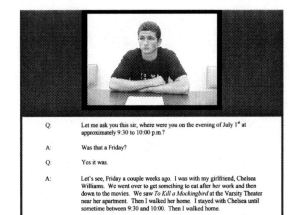

Lawrence video +   **Slide 82**

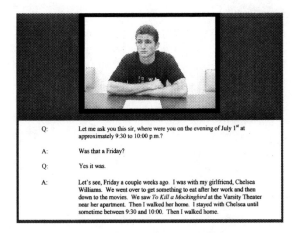

Lawrence video +   **Slide 83**

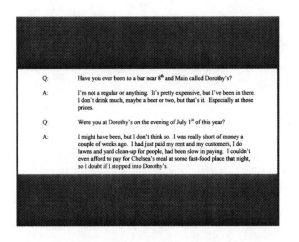

Have you ever?   **Slide 84**

Easy Tech: Cases and Materials on Courtroom Technology
© The National Institute for Trial Advocacy

Lawrence video **Slide 85**

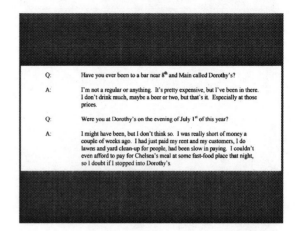

Q: Have you ever been to a bar near 8th and Main called Dorothy's?

A: I'm not a regular or anything. It's pretty expensive, but I've been in there. I don't drink much, maybe a beer or two, but that's it. Especially at those prices.

Q: Were you at Dorothy's on the evening of July 1st of this year?

A: I might have been, but I don't think so. I was really short of money a couple of weeks ago. I had just paid my rent and my customers, I do lawns and yard clean-up for people, had been slow in paying. I couldn't even afford to pay for Chelsea's meal at some fast-food place that night, so I doubt if I stopped into Dorothy's.

Lawrence have you reveal **Slide 86**

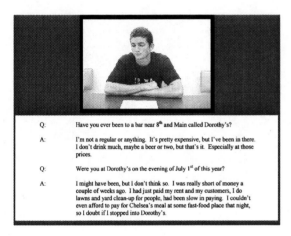

Q: Have you ever been to a bar near 8th and Main called Dorothy's?

A: I'm not a regular or anything. It's pretty expensive, but I've been in there. I don't drink much, maybe a beer or two, but that's it. Especially at those prices.

Q: Were you at Dorothy's on the evening of July 1st of this year?

A: I might have been, but I don't think so. I was really short of money a couple of weeks ago. I had just paid my rent and my customers, I do lawns and yard clean-up for people, had been slow in paying. I couldn't even afford to pay for Chelsea's meal at some fast-food place that night, so I doubt if I stopped into Dorothy's.

Lawrence video + **Slide 87**

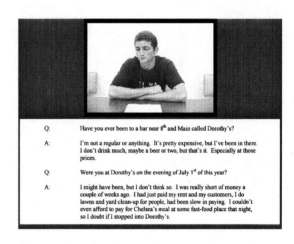

Q: Have you ever been to a bar near 8th and Main called Dorothy's?

A: I'm not a regular or anything. It's pretty expensive, but I've been in there. I don't drink much, maybe a beer or two, but that's it. Especially at those prices.

Q: Were you at Dorothy's on the evening of July 1st of this year?

A: I might have been, but I don't think so. I was really short of money a couple of weeks ago. I had just paid my rent and my customers, I do lawns and yard clean-up for people, had been slow in paying. I couldn't even afford to pay for Chelsea's meal at some fast-food place that night, so I doubt if I stopped into Dorothy's.

Lawrence video + **Slide 88**

Officer Wright:	The time is 5:18 p.m., the date July 16th. We are in the Nita City Police Department conference room with Ms. Gale Fitzgerald. Ms. Fitzgerald, we're videotaping this session with your knowledge and permission, is that correct?
Ms. Fitzgerald:	Yes, that's true.
Officer Wright:	We've again asked you to come to the station to help us in our investigation of the mugging that took place on July 1st in which you were the victim. We have several photographs we'd like to show you. Please tell us if any of these five photos is of the man who attacked you and took your purse.
Ms. Fitzgerald:	Why yes, that's him, number 4. Oh yes, how did you know? What's his name? Has he done this before to others?
Officer Wright:	I can't tell you ma'am any details about our investigation. Are you certain this is the man who attacked you on July 1st?
Ms. Fitzgerald:	Well, I wouldn't put my life on it, it was dark you know, but I definitely recognize the tattoo on his right arm. His arm was right next to me. The face, there was barely enough light for me to see his face, and it was only for a few seconds. This looks like the guy. No, I'm sure this is the guy. It must be.
Officer Wright:	That you very much, Ms. Fitzgerald. We'll be letting you know when you're needed for trial. Off record.

Fitzgerald statement **Slide 89**

Fitzgerald video **Slide 90**

Easy Tech: Cases and Materials on Courtroom Technology
© The National Institute for Trial Advocacy

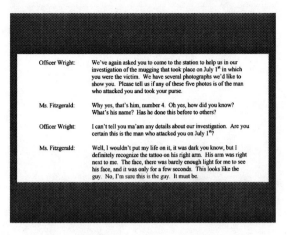

Fitzgerald Q & A's   **Slide 91**

Fitzgerald video   **Slide 92**

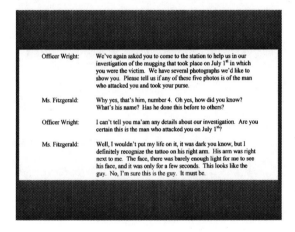

Q & A reveal   **Slide 93**

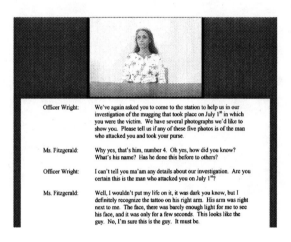

Fitzgerald video +   **Slide 94**

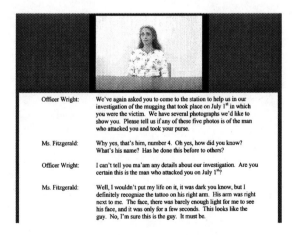

Fitzgerald video +   **Slide 95**

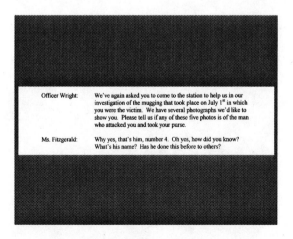

Fitzgerald Q & A   **Slide 96**

Easy Tech: Cases and Materials on Courtroom Technology
© The National Institute for Trial Advocacy

Fitzgerald video **Slide 97**

Fitzgerald Q & A reveal **Slide 98**

Fitzgerald video + **Slide 99**

Fitzgerald video + **Slide 100**

Fitzgerald Q & A **Slide 101**

Fitzgerald Q & A video **Slide 102**

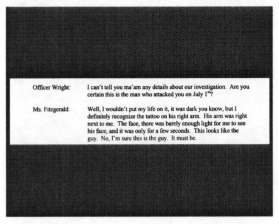

Fitzgerald Q & A reveal **Slide 103**

Fitzgerald video + **Slide 104**

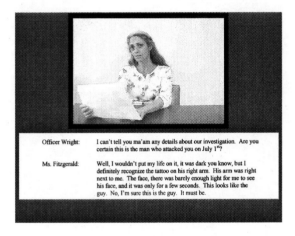

Fitzgerald video + **Slide 105**

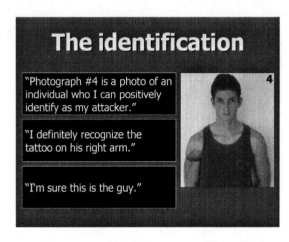

The identification **Slide 106**

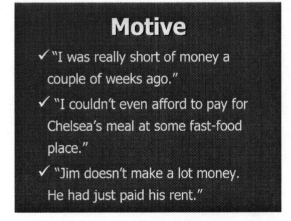

Motive **Slide 107**

Photos shown **Slide 108**

Easy Tech: Cases and Materials on Courtroom Technology
© The National Institute for Trial Advocacy

Chelsea Williams
Alibi witness???

Mugging just after 9:45 on Friday, July 1st

Not sure if movie 6/30 or 7/1

Home between 9:15 & 9:30

He stayed 10-15 minutes

DF says left 9:30 – 10:00

No more than 10 minute walk

Chelsea Williams   **Slide 109**

State must prove:

- On or about July 1, YR-1
- Property taken from Fitzgerald
- By force & against her will
- Pushed & thrown to ground
- Defendant did it

State must prove   **Slide 110**

Scene

- July 1st, 9:45 p.m.
- Lighting:
  - Only at intersections
  - Some small porch lights
  - Big, leafy trees whole block
- Sidewalk, mid-block

Scene   **Slide 111**

Identification

- Happened in less than 15 seconds
- 5' 8" – 5' 10"
- 160 – 175 pounds
- Dark hair
- Dark pants
- 10/3 – Shown photo, no ID

Identification   **Slide 112**

Gayle Fitzgerald

- Long week
- Preparing for trial
- Friday night
- Long day
- Left at 9:15 p.m.
- Middle of block
- "It was dark"

- From behind
- Before could turn
- Struggle for purse
- Money & valuables
- Only a few seconds
- Very upset
- Can't put life on it

Gayle Fitzgerald   **Slide 113**

Beyond a Reasonable Doubt

BARD   **Slide 114**

Easy Tech: Cases and Materials on Courtroom Technology
© The National Institute for Trial Advocacy

Shown mug books   **Slide 115**

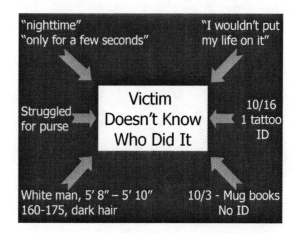

Victim doesn't know   **Slide 116**

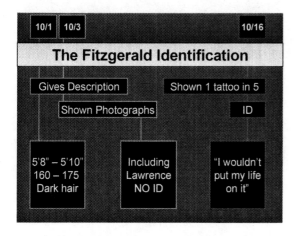

The Fitzgerald ID   **Slide 117**

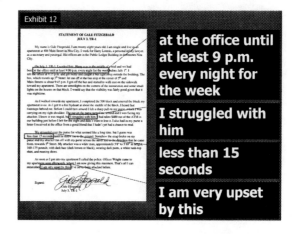

Exhibit 12   **Slide 118**

Easy Tech: Cases and Materials on Courtroom Technology
© The National Institute for Trial Advocacy

PROBLEM 1
(Exhibits: Defendant's statement)

For the State, introduce the statement of James Lawrence (Exhibit 5) in evidence. When showing the proposed exhibit to the court, opposing counsel, and the witness for foundational purposes, utilize the electronic form of the exhibit. Assume the judge can prevent the jury from viewing the exhibit until it is introduced in evidence.

For the Defendant, oppose the offer.

PROBLEM 2
(Exhibits: Victim's statement)

For the Defendant, introduce the statement of Gail Fitzgerald (Exhibit 2) in evidence. When showing the exhibit to the court, opposing counsel, and the witness for foundational purposes, utilize the electronic form of the exhibit. Assume the judge can prevent the jury from viewing the exhibit until it is introduced in evidence.

PROBLEM 3
(Exhibits: Photo)

For the State, introduce the photo of the mugging scene (Exhibit 17) in evidence and make use of it in the direct examination of Fitzgerald, utilizing the evidence camera as the display device.

For the Defendant, oppose the offer and use.

PROBLEM 4
(Exhibits: Photo)

For the Defendant, introduce the photo of the mugging scene (Exhibit 19) in evidence and make use of it in the cross-examination of Fitzgerald, utilizing the evidence camera as the display device.

For the State, oppose the offer and use.

Easy Tech: Cases and Materials on Courtroom Technology
© The National Institute for Trial Advocacy

PROBLEM 5
(Direct examination with illustrative aid: Main Street map)

For the State, conduct the direct examination of Fitzgerald regarding the mugging utilizing the map of Main Street (Exhibit 10) as an illustrative aid.

Part A: Use the evidence camera and the marking pen as your display device during the examination.

Part B: Use the computer and the telestrator as your display device during the examination.

For the Defendant, oppose the offer and use in Parts A and B.

PROBLEM 6
(Direct examination with illustrative aid: Nita City map)

For the Defendant, conduct the direct examination of Lawrence utilizing the grid map of Nita City (Exhibit 9) as an illustrative aid.

Part A: Use the evidence camera and marking pen as the display device during your examination.

Part B: Use the computer and the telestrator as the display device during your examination.

For the State, oppose the offer and use in Parts A and B.

PROBLEM 7
(Direct examination with exhibit: Defendant's statement)

For the State, conduct the direct examination of Officer Wright regarding the admissions of James Lawrence, utilizing the Statement of Lawrence (Exhibit 5) during your examination. For the purposes of this problem, assume that Exhibit 5 has been admitted in evidence.

Part A: Use the evidence camera and marking pen as the display device during your examination.

Part B: Use the computer and telestrator as the display device during your examination.

Part C: Use the computer slide show with callouts and bullet points (PowerPoint slides 14–17) as the display device during your examination.

For the Defendant, oppose the offer and use in Parts A, B, and C.

Easy Tech: Cases and Materials on Courtroom Technology
© The National Institute for Trial Advocacy

PROBLEM 8
(Cross-examination with exhibit: Victim's statement)

For the Defendant, conduct the cross-examination of Fitzgerald concerning her identification of Lawrence, utilizing her statement (Exhibit 2). For the purposes of this problem, assume that Exhibit 2 has been admitted in evidence.

Part A: Use the evidence camera and marking pen as the display device during your examination.

Part B: Use the computer and telestrator as the display device during your examination.

Part C: Use the computer slide show with callouts and bullet points (PowerPoint slides 10–12) as the display device during your examination.

For the State, oppose the offer and use in Parts A, B, and C.

PROBLEM 9
(Impeachment using transcript/video excerpt: Fitzgerald)

On direct examination the victim, Gale Fitzgerald, has testified as follows: "I didn't have any trouble at all identifying my attacker once I was shown those five photos. I'd have recognized that face anywhere."

For the Defendant, conduct the impeachment of Fitzgerald.

Part A: Conduct the impeachment of Fitzgerald utilizing whatever portions you choose of the transcript of her July 16th statement to Officer Wright that appears in this volume.

Part B: Conduct the impeachment of Fitzgerald utilizing whatever portions you choose of her July 16th statement to Officer Wright which appears in the PowerPoint slide show on your CD.

Part C: Conduct the impeachment of Fitzgerald utilizing whatever portions you choose of the videotape of her July 16th statement to Officer Wright with the entirety or reveal of the written transcript appearing beneath it, which appears in the PowerPoint slide show on your CD.

For the Prosecution, oppose the impeachment and the use cf exhibits in Parts A, B, and C.

Easy Tech: Cases and Materials on Courtroom Technology
© The National Institute for Trial Advocacy

PROBLEM 10
(Impeachment using transcript/video excerpt: Lawrence)

On direct examination the Defendant, James Lawrence, has testified as follows: "I am certain I stayed with Chelsea until 10 P.M. because I remember the 10 o'clock news coming on just before I left."

For the Prosecution, conduct the impeachment of Lawrence.

Part A: Conduct the impeachment of Lawrence utilizing whatever portions you choose of the transcript of his statement to Officer Wright that appears in this volume.

Part B: Conduct the impeachment of Lawrence utilizing whatever portions you choose of his statement to Officer Wright which appear on your CD.

Part C: Conduct the impeachment of Lawrence utilizing whatever portions you choose of the videotape of his statement to Officer Wright with the entirety or reveal of the written transcript appearing beneath it, which appears in the PowerPoint slide show on your CD.

For the Defendant, oppose the impeachment and the use of exhibits in Parts A, B, and C.

For the purposes of Problems 11–14, you need not go through a formal foundation before exhibits can be offered in evidence. Simply make the offer and be prepared to argue admissibility based on the facts in the file should there be an objection.

PROBLEM 11
(Direct and cross-examination: Fitzgerald)

For the State, conduct the direct examination of Gail Fitzgerald, utilizing the exhibits and illustrative aids available in the file of your own choosing.

For the Defendant, conduct the cross-examination of Fitzgerald, utilizing the exhibits and illustrative aids available in the file of your own choosing.

PROBLEM 12
(Direct and cross-examination: Williams)

For the Defendant, conduct the direct examination of Chelsea Williams, utilizing the exhibits and illustrative aids available in the file of your choosing.

For the State, conduct the cross-examination of Williams, utilizing the exhibits and illustrative aids available in the file of your choosing.

Easy Tech: Cases and Materials on Courtroom Technology
© The National Institute for Trial Advocacy

PROBLEM 13
(Direct and cross-examination: Wright)

For the State, conduct the direct examination of Officer Wright, utilizing the exhibits and illustrative aids available in the file of your choosing.

For the Defendants, conduct the cross-examination of Wright, utilizing the exhibits and illustrative aids available in the file of your choosing.

PROBLEM 14
(Direct and cross-examination: Lawrence)

For the Defendant, conduct the direct examination of James Lawrence, utilizing the exhibits and illustrative aids available in the file of your choosing.

For the State, conduct the cross-examination of Lawrence, utilizing the exhibits and illustrative aids available in the file of your choosing.

PROBLEM 15
(Opening statement)

Prepare a ten-minute portion of the opening statement for your client in the case of *State v. Lawrence*. Assume the trial judge has ruled that you may utilize any evidentiary exhibit (in hard copy or in electronic form, displayed in the manner of your own choosing) in the case, during the opening statement. Any illustrative aids, either from the file or of your own creation, must be shown to your opponent who will have an opportunity to make objections for the judge's ruling. A brief hearing on the use of illustrative aids will be conducted. The hearing does not count toward the ten-minute portion of the opening statement assigned by the problem.

PROBLEM 16
(Closing argument)

Prepare a fifteen-minute portion of the closing argument for your client in the case of *State v. Lawrence*. In performing this exercise you may utilize any admissible evidentiary exhibit. In addition, you must use **at least** one illustrative aid from the file or of your own creation. The evidentiary exhibits and illustrative aids may be displayed in any form, utilizing the display device of your choosing. The choice and use of exhibits and illustrative aids will be one of the points of critique for this exercise.

Easy Tech: Cases and Materials on Courtroom Technology
© The National Institute for Trial Advocacy

PROBLEM 17
(Defense Opening and Closing)

For the purposes of **this problem only**, assume the defense investigator tracked down two of the other men whose photos appear in Exhibit 14 and took photographs of each of them wearing tank tops. These two photos marked as Exhibits 22 and 23, along with a separate PowerPoint slide show, are on the CD in a folder labeled Problem 17.

Part A: For the Defendant, prepare a portion of an opening statement based on these additional facts, exhibits, and illustrative aids.

Part B: For the Defendant, prepare a portion of a closing argument based on these additional facts, exhibits, and illustrative aids.

Brown v. Byrd
Personal Injury Case

Brown v. Byrd
Contents

Easy Tech: Cases and Materials on Courtroom Technology
© The National Institute for Trial Advocacy

Exhibit 15. Diagram of intersection, labeled

Exhibit 16. Photo of Brown's vehicle

Exhibit 17. Photo of Byrd's vehicle

Exhibit 18. Plaintiff's Complaint, p. 3

Exhibit 19. Medical report, David McCullough

Exhibit 20. Video clip, Brown depo., p. 17 (on the CD)

Exhibit 21. Video clip, Brown depo., p. 49 (on the CD)

Exhibit 22. Video clip, Byrd depo., p. 18 (on the CD)

Exhibit 23. Video clip, Byrd depo., p. 35 (on the CD)

Exhibit 24. Thumbnails of evidentiary exhibits and illustrative aids

Thumbnails of Slides

PART V: Brown v. Byrd[1]

Fact Summary

Kenneth Brown brought suit against Robert Byrd for damages arising out of a collision between their cars on April 20, YR-1[2], near the intersection of 12th Avenue and East Main Street in Nita City. Brown alleges that Byrd was following him too closely and failed to keep a proper lookout. Brown is seeking to recover damages in excess of $250,000 for his neck, back, and closed-head injuries, which he claims were caused by Byrd's negligence. Byrd denies liability and asserts that the impact was caused when Brown stopped short after initially starting through the intersection, and in the alternative, even if the accident was his fault, the impact was not sufficient to cause, and did not cause, any physical injury to Brown.

The accident was investigated at the scene by Officer David Pierce of the Nita City Police Department. Officer Pierce was called to the scene of this accident by radio dispatch at 3:40 p.m. and conducted an investigation. He interviewed the two drivers involved in the accident and inspected the scene. The accident was, in his opinion, unavoidable. That, coupled with the fact that there were no injuries either visible or complained of by either party, resulted in no citations being issued for this accident.

Brown alleges that as a result of being rear-ended by Byrd's car he suffered a back injury. He further claims that the injury precludes him from engaging in any strenuous exercise or activity, and that the muscle relaxant prescription drugs he is required to take prevent him from drinking any alcoholic beverages, even beer. Brown asserts that his back injury, and the pain and suffering from his back and head injuries, and the deprivation of his activities warrant substantial compensation. Brown is also asking for lost wages.

Byrd's insurance carrier asked one of its investigators, David Randolf, to review and verify Brown's alleged injuries. After an investigation, Randolf filed a report with the insurance carrier disputing the extent of the injuries claimed by Brown. Randolf began his investigation by identifying Brown by reference to a picture provided by the insurance company and by setting up a surveillance of Brown's home on June 24, YR-1. He noted no unusual activity on the first day of the surveillance. On June 25, Randolf followed Brown to the Nita Country Club. This was just over two months after Brown's alleged injury. At that time, Randolf observed Brown play two sets of tennis and then consume four or five beers, both at the tennis court and at the nearby outdoor patio bar. Randolf took photographs of Brown playing tennis and drinking afterwards.

---

1. The *Brown v. Byrd* case is adapted from *Problems in Trial Advocacy*, NITA 1996, by Bocchino and Beskind, and also appeared in *Problems and Cases in Trial Advocacy*, Volume 1, CLE Edition, NITA 1982, by Bocchino, Beskind, Broun, and Seckinger.

2. NITA uses a convention for dates as follows: YR-0 (this year), YR-1 (last year), YR-2 (two years ago), and so on. Students should use the actual dates in working on the exercises.

Easy Tech: Cases and Materials on Courtroom Technology
© The National Institute for Trial Advocacy

DEPOSITION SUMMARY OF KENNETH BROWN

My name is Ken Brown and I am thirty-three years old. I am single. For the past five years I have worked as an institutional stockbroker here in Nita City at Golden Investments, located at 637 12th Avenue. I live at 5 Scott Place in the southern part of town. I grew up here and graduated from South Central Nita High School. I was on the swim team and the tennis team while in high school and concentrated on tennis while in college, competing on the collegiate level at UCLA where I played both singles and doubles. Even though I was not good enough to turn pro, tennis played a big part in my life after that, not only because I like the game and it helps me keep in shape, but also because it opened a lot of doors for me professionally in landing accounts and keeping customers happy. I joined the Nita Country Club, in fact, soon after taking my current position with Golden Investments.

I was driving home at the time of the accident. I had left work at the same time as usual. I have to be at work before 6 a.m. because the stock market opens at 9:30 a.m. East Coast time, which is 6:30 a.m. out here. Walt Wilkins, who handles after-hours trading, came in about 2 p.m. to cover me and I briefed him about where the market stood when it closed at 4 p.m. East Coast time and what we traded up to that point. I have known Walt since college—he was my doubles partner on the tennis team. At any rate, I left shortly after 3:00 or so. My office is just six blocks up 12th Avenue from Main Street and I take the same route every day when I head home. I am always especially careful as I near Main Street because the elementary school is right on the corner and a lot of youngsters are out and about at the school using the playground all year-round. On the day of the accident the school was just letting out at around 3:15 or 3:30, and there were a lot of kids out. There were also some crossing guards, and I think there was an ice cream truck on one corner of the intersection. As I approached the intersection I was extra cautious with the kids in the area. Because the light was green, I intended to go through the intersection.

I was traveling south at no more than twenty miles per hour as I approached the intersection. Just before I got to the crosswalk, the light turned yellow. Because I travel this same street five days a week, I know this light has an especially quick yellow. At the same time I saw a kid running towards the intersection near the crossing guard. Because of the shortness of the yellow light and the kid, I knew I would never be able to safely make it through the intersection, so I applied my brakes and stopped almost immediately. I didn't realize the clown behind me had speeded up from a safe distance behind me to right on my tail, and the instant I stopped, he smashed into my car.

<u>Page 17</u>

1. Q. Where was your car, in relation to the crosswalk, when you were hit?

2. A. I had just come up to the crosswalk.

3. Q. No part of your car was in the crosswalk at all?

4. A. I was just into the crosswalk when I got smashed, but he pushed me through the

Easy Tech: Cases and Materials on Courtroom Technology
© The National Institute for Trial Advocacy

5.   crosswalk and into the intersection.

6.   Q.   Where was the front of your car in relation to the crosswalk when you got out of

7.   the car?

8.   A.   I was just through the crosswalk into the intersection.

9.   Q.   How far did your car move forward after you were hit from behind?

10.   A.   I'm not sure, the width of the crosswalk, maybe 10 feet.

I will draw on this diagram you have given me the approximate location my Honda was when it was hit from behind. I drew a rectangle and put the word "Honda" written beside it. I also drew in the Volvo. I have also shown where I saw the kid and the crossing guard by marking it with an X. I have marked that as Exhibit 12 as you requested.

I didn't feel hurt at all after the accident. It's funny how you hear about other people in accidents who feel fine with the rush of adrenalin right afterwards, and only later start to feel bad. That's what happened to me. The police officer was there in a matter of minutes and I told him I felt fine and didn't need any medical assistance. It was obvious who was at fault because the other guy rear-ended me. When it came time to explaining what actually happened, the officer didn't have time for us. He spent ten minutes getting down all the basic information like name, address, license numbers and so on, but then he got called to another accident and left. We never got to tell him what happened. I was shocked that he didn't give Byrd a ticket. He just rushed off without fully investigating our accident. He seemed like a real rookie, too. Nice enough guy, but still wet behind the ears, if you know what I mean. He couldn't have been older than twenty or twenty-one.

The next day my neck and back got worse and worse. I was in so much pain, I had to see my doctor, Dr. Gomez. He sent me to the hospital to get an X-ray and an MRI. I was told that they didn't show anything other than some degenerated disc problems at L4–5. The doctor told me that this was probably from years of playing tennis and probably not from the accident. He said that there was little he could do for me, and recommended that I rest and take ibuprofen for pain. I decided I'd see a chiropractor, Dr. McCullough, who has an office in his house near my home. Dr. McCullough recommended we treat the condition conservatively, meaning with regular adjustments, hot baths, ibuprofen, and massage for the first week. When this didn't do much to relieve the pain that first week, he then prescribed the muscle relaxants that I've been taking ever since just to marginally function. I also got a prescription for pain medication for when it just got too much to handle, but I use them sparingly. I also had some really bad headaches for a few weeks and got dizzy spells for a short time. The headaches came on about every afternoon. I only get a headache now about once a week.

It was very difficult for me mentally as well, trying to handle the loss of my physical life, and wondering if my back problem would ever go away so I could feel normal again. The nights were the worst time because I found it hard to find a comfortable position and I didn't sleep nearly as soundly as I used to. And I would wake up stiff as a board, and have to take pills all day to make it through. At the suggestion of my lawyer, I kept a diary about how I was feeling. (That diary was produced at the deposition as Exhibit 2.) In the past two months I have had some improvement and although I still can't play tennis, I can do the stretching I used to do religiously every morning, and I'm getting better. My back gave me problems at work as well. I often had to work standing up. Since I've been stretching regularly in the past several months, I've been okay at work. I do get tired a lot faster than I used to. By the end of work, it's all I can do to get home and put my feet up to rest. I am hopeful that I'll be able to start playing tennis again in the future. Dr. McCullough says I've made progress and if I continue my treatments, tennis is not out of the question, although I'll probably never get back to the level I was at before the accident. Overall, I'd say my back is about 80 percent of what it was before the accident. The real problems lasted for about six months, and since then I've been making pretty steady progress.

Page 49

1.   Q.   Do you drink alcohol?

2.   A.   Not now I don't.

3.   Q.   What about before the accident, did you drink then?

4.   A.   Well, I never have much been a big drinker, I would have an occasional beer or two

5.   after work with a client or friend, or often after playing tennis, or wine with a date.

6.   Nothing much.

7.   Q.   Would you drink three or four beers in one get-together?

8.   A.   No, just one or two at the most.

9.   Q.   After the accident, did you drink at all?

10.   A.   No, that's been cut out of my life as well because of strict orders from my

11.   doctor not to mix alcohol with my medications.

12.   Q.   Have you followed those orders exactly at all times?

13.   A.   I followed those orders to a tee. I don't drink at all anymore, not even beer.

14.   Q.   You never drink anything alcoholic now, not even a beer or two?

15.   A.   No, I don't. I can't drink so much as a single beer on this medication.

Yes, these photos marked as Exhibits 4, 5, 6, and 7 are pictures of me playing tennis. I recognize the court as one at the country club. Yes, these photos marked as Exhibits 8, 9 and 10 are pictures of me drinking a beer. Exhibit 11 looks like just outside on the courts. Also at the club. So what. Who took these? I have no idea when they were taken. They couldn't have been taken since the accident because, like I said, I haven't been able to play tennis or drink beer.

No, you're right, there was that one time just a couple months after the accident when I foolishly tried to see if I could handle a game of tennis. I was so frustrated that I just had to try and play, I missed it so much. I played with my doubles partner, Walter Wilkins, who I also work with. I took a bunch of muscle relaxants and I felt okay during the couple of sets we played. I was so excited I probably had a few beers just to celebrate being back out on the courts and feeling so alive. Walt had driven, so I wasn't worried about driving home. And did I pay for it later that day and for a couple of weeks after that. My chiropractor was really upset with me and said I probably set my treatment back a month. But that was the one and only time I tested myself that way. I learned my lesson the hard way.

This accident has also hurt me financially. I was not as good at my job during YR-1 because I was distracted by pain. I was the top earner in my group in YR-2 and I made a little over $250,000. In YR-1, I was eighteenth out of twenty people in the group and made over $60,000 less than in YR-2. My income for YR-1 was approximately $190,000, as compared to $250,000 in YR-2. Fortunately I have been feeling better this year and my earnings are back up, so I'm currently second in the group for YR-0.

You have shown me a notebook marked as Exhibit 2 and I recognize it as a diary I kept of times when I felt pain after the accident. It isn't complete because I didn't start it until I was advised to do so two weeks after the accident by my lawyer, and I wasn't always diligent in making notes. You have also shown me a document marked as Exhibit 3. I recognize Exhibit 3 as the first quarter YR-1 work evaluation I received at my job at Golden Investments. I don't agree with the evaluation, but it is what I received from my supervisor, Alyssa Hoffman.

I have read this deposition, and it is complete and accurate.

Kenneth Brown
_____
Kenneth Brown
November 15, YR-1

DEPOSITION SUMMARY OF ROBERT BYRD

My name is Bob Byrd. I am thirty-five years old and I live at 104 East Main Street in Nita City. I am married with two children, Mike, age eight, and David, age six. I work as a salesperson for an auto parts supply company, Nita Automart. I have been sued by Kenneth Brown for a car accident I had with him.

Page 18

1.   Q: Where were you going at the time of the accident?

2.   A: I had an appointment at Ferguson Auto Body.

3.   Q: Where is that located?

4.   A: In South Nita City.

5.   Q: What time was the appointment?

6.   A: Four.

7.   Q: Why were you going there?

8.   A: They're a client of mine. I had an appointment to meet with the Parts Manager,

9.   Bill Cheswick. He's hard to get an appointment with.

10. Q: How long does it take to get to Ferguson's from where the accident happened?

11. A: I know I was cutting it close, but if it wouldn't have been for this accident, I would

12. have gotten there in time.

As I said, the accident involved a man, who I now know as Ken Brown, at the intersection of 12th and East Main in Nita City on April 20, YR-1. The accident occurred at 3:30 in the afternoon. The weather was clear and dry.

As I approached the intersection of 12th and Main, I was traveling south on 12th Avenue at about 25 mph which is the speed limit on that part of 12th Avenue. Mr. Brown's Honda sedan was about two car lengths ahead of me.

The light was green but Brown slowed a bit as he came to the intersection. On the northwest corner of that intersection is the Nita Elementary School. Because school was letting out at that time, I was being especially careful watching the schoolchildren near the intersection on the northwest corner. I saw a crossing guard bending over and talking to a little boy, who looked like my David, on the northeast corner of the intersection. There were also some children, I'd estimate about eight or ten of them, crowded around an ice cream truck parked just east of the intersection, facing west on East Main Street.

1. Q: Tell me how the accident happened.

2. A: I was driving behind Mr. Brown's car, maybe fifteen feet behind him, going

3. no more than twenty. When I got about twenty feet from the crosswalk on 12th, the light

4. turned yellow. By then I was ten feet behind him because he had slowed some.

5. I look up, and his brake lights were off and he seemed to be speeding up,

6. so I assumed Mr. Brown would continue through the intersection.

7. Q: Where was Mr. Brown's car at the time the light turned yellow?

8. A: Just into the crosswalk.

9. Q: Not into the intersection?

10. A: Well just about.

11. Q: But not there yet?

12. A: Not yet, but I assumed he would continue through.

13. Q: Why did you make that assumption?

14. A: It was the only intelligent thing to do.

15. Q: Why's that?

16. A: Well, otherwise he would have to have jammed on his brakes and stop

17. suddenly.

18. Q: What's wrong with that?

19. A: Obviously, it can cause someone following behind to run into you.

20. Q: Which is what you did?

21. A: My point exactly.

22. Q: Had Mr. Brown continued as you assumed, what were you going

23.   to do?

24.   A: I planned to follow him right through the intersection. In my opinion, it was safer

25.   to go through the light, even if it changed while I was in the intersection, than jamming

26.   on my brakes.

26.   Q: Even if the light turned red?

28.   A: Yes, even if it turned red.

At any rate, I glanced left and right as I got to the intersection. Instead of going through, Brown suddenly slammed on the brakes and stopped. He must have been almost through the crosswalk when he braked. That's why I thought he was going through. I hit the brakes as hard as I could, but I still ran into the rear end of Brown's car. I have marked on this diagram the location of Brown's car and the location of my car when the impact happened. I'm sure Brown was through the crosswalk and into the intersection when I hit him. I may not have these exactly to scale, though. I marked this as Exhibit 13 and I signed it as you have asked. When I hit him, I was doing no more than 10 mph. In fact, the damage to my car, a YR-1 Volvo, was minimal. There was a hardly noticeable ding in the back of Brown's Honda. The impact was so minimal that neither of our air bags inflated.

Brown jumped out of his car and came towards me. I asked him why he stopped short, and he said he had a red light and the wreck was all my fault. I didn't want to get into an argument with him, so I didn't respond, but to my way of thinking, this accident was his fault. It is unsafe to stop so quickly. The yellow light is a caution light, not a stop light, and he should have driven appropriately and gone through the intersection with caution especially when he didn't brake until the last possible second after he was in the crosswalk. I did ask him if he was hurt and he said that he wasn't.

A cop came and investigated the accident. I told him I couldn't avoid hitting Brown. He obviously agreed with me because I didn't get a ticket.

I have read this deposition, and it is complete and accurate.

Robert Byrd

_____
Robert Byrd
November 18, YR-1

Easy Tech: Cases and Materials on Courtroom Technology
© The National Institute for Trial Advocacy

DEPOSITION SUMMARY OF OFFICER DAVID PIERCE

I am David Pierce, patrol officer for the Nita City Police Department. I am twenty-three years old and have been on the force two years. On April 20, YR-1, I received a dispatch at approximately 3:40 p.m. to proceed to the intersection of 12th Avenue and East Main for a reported accident. I arrived within five minutes and noted a two-car, rear-end collision in the southbound lane of 12th Avenue at around the north crosswalk. The drivers of the two cars, whom I later identified to be Kenneth Brown and Robert Byrd, were standing on the sidewalk by the elementary school. I first spoke with the drivers to determine the extent of any injuries in order to decide whether an ambulance would be necessary. Neither appeared injured nor did either complain of injuries. Both were cooperative and reasonably calm. No ambulance was called.

I then surveyed the accident itself, noting that a Volvo sedan driven by Mr. Byrd had struck the rear bumper of a Honda sedan driven by Mr. Brown. Both vehicles were driveable. It was a clear, sunny day. I made notes of the standard information such as license plate and vehicle registration, date and time, insurance coverage, home addresses.

Then, as I was about to interview each driver separately, I received a message from dispatch that a twenty-car chain-reaction pileup had just occurred on the nearby Interstate, where there were several serious injuries reported, and I was directed to proceed to location ASAP. As a result, I left the scene without fully investigating the accident, and only took brief statements from each driver. I did not actually prepare my official accident report until the following day since most of my time for the rest of my shift and beyond was taken up with the accident on the Interstate.

What I recall of the driver statements is consistent with what I noted in my report. Exhibit 1 is that report. As Mr. Brown approached the intersection on a green light, it reportedly changed to yellow. I know from my own experience that the light at that intersection has a quick yellow, but there's no way to know that unless you've been there numerous times. I am not sure exactly where he said he was located when that happened. What I do remember is Mr. Brown conveying was that he decided to stop rather than proceed through the intersection on a yellow light. No, he did not say anything about a child running towards the crosswalk. If he had, I'm sure I would recall that. Mr. Byrd was reportedly driving at or below the speed limit of 25 miles per hour when in his view Mr. Brown suddenly and without warning came to a rapid stop. Mr. Byrd had assumed that Brown would be going through the intersection because he did not have his brake lights on as he was going into the crosswalk area. Byrd couldn't stop fast enough, and his front bumper struck the rear bumper of Brown's car. Damage was minimal, which further corroborated the slow speed of the Byrd vehicle. Brown's car ended up in the intersection.

Yes, I realize that the driver behind in such situations is usually considered at fault. I did not issue any citations in part because the damage was slight, neither party seemed injured, and while Mr. Byrd may have been following closer than is prudent, Mr. Brown made the accident unavoidable by stopping when it appeared to me from what I heard that he should have continued through the intersection. Also, after hearing about the accident on the Interstate, I simply needed to finish up with my investigation and proceed as rapidly as possible to what was obviously a more urgent situation. Perhaps if I would have had more time to talk with the parties and weigh the situation, I might have issued a citation to Mr. Byrd, but I doubt it.

Neither party showed any signs of intoxication and thus that was categorically ruled out as a possible cause of the accident. I don't recall what Mr. Byrd looked like, but I do remember Mr. Brown somewhat because he was tall, lanky, and looked like a real jock. What I mean is he had the body of an athlete.

Yes, this diagram that has been marked as Exhibit 14 looks like the intersection back when this accident took place and accurately shows where the crosswalks are. Since you've asked me to draw in where the two cars ended up as I saw them when I arrived, I have drawn a box and put the letter "H" for the Honda driven by Mr. Brown, and another box behind it with the letter "V" for the Volvo driven by Mr. Byrd. I believe this drawing accurately shows where the cars were relative to the crosswalk on 12th Avenue when I arrived. Of course, I am only going from memory because I didn't make a drawing or sketch at the scene. So I may be a little off here.

I have read this deposition, and it is complete and accurate.

David Pierce

David Pierce
November 19, YR-1

DEPOSITION SUMMARY OF DAVID RANDOLF

My name is David Randolf. I am forty-three years old and work as an investigator for the Nita Insurance Company. The biggest lines of insurance our company writes are auto, fire, and casualty. My job for the past six years has been to investigate claims made under such policies by and against our insureds. In this capacity I was asked to conduct a surveillance of Kenneth Brown, who was involved in an automobile collision with one such insured named Robert Byrd, to review and verify the alleged injuries. I was told Mr. Brown was claiming to have seriously injured his back as a result of a rear-end collision in downtown Nita on April 20, YR-1. Apparently he claimed to be an avid tennis player and that the accident had caused such back pain that he was unable to play tennis. To assist in this investigation, I was provided with a photograph of a man I was told was Mr. Brown.

I set up a surveillance at Mr. Brown's home address, 5 Scott Place, on June 24, YR-1. No unusual activity was noted that day. On June 25 Mr. Brown left his house carrying what appeared to be a covered tennis racket and got in a car I now know to belong to a Walter Wilkins. I followed him to the Nita Country Club out in Nita Heights. After a time in the locker room, Mr. Brown reappeared in tennis clothing, and carrying that same racket, headed out to the tennis courts adjacent to the clubhouse. I took up position in the bushes next to the court on which he was playing, as shown in the photograph you have just shown me, which is marked as Exhibit 11. My intent was to see without being seen. I had my small but powerful digital zoom camera with me to take pictures of any significant activity. The camera is capable of taking digital video as well, but I did not use that function in this surveillance.

I watched Mr. Brown play two vigorous sets of tennis and managed to take a few pictures of him in action at various stages of the game. He seemed to move effortlessly about the court, never showing any signs of stiffness or pain. I could overhear the conversations between Mr. Brown and his opponent and while he complained of being rusty, Mr. Brown never complained of pain or impairment at all. He looked very athletic as he glided about the court, firing serves, bending for volleys, and stretching for overhead smashes. I myself have played recreational tennis for several years and am very familiar with the sport. Mr. Brown is obviously a very accomplished tennis player. If he had any back problems as of that date, it sure didn't show during the forty or so minutes I watched him play.

When I realized the second set was near to being done, I moved to another location to avoid being spotted by Mr. Brown. After the match, Mr. Brown drank one or two beers at courtside, which I noted with a photograph, and then he and his playing partner went to the club's outdoor patio bar, where I saw him drink another three or four beers. I also took a photograph of him drinking at the bar. The photos were taken because in my experience people with the back pain that Mr. Brown claimed to have are required to take medications that don't mix with alcohol. I again detected no signs of pain, stress, discomfort, and the like.

The eight photographs you have shown me, marked as Exhibits 4, 5, 6, 7, 8, 9, 10, and 11 are all ones I took that day. I kept the diskette used to record the photos and delivered a hard copy of the photos to the lawyer for Mr. Byrd. I did enhance the contrast of the photos before

Easy Tech: Cases and Materials on Courtroom Technology
© The National Institute for Trial Advocacy

printing them, but nonetheless each photo is a true and accurate representation of what I saw that day.

I have read this deposition, and it is complete and accurate.

David Randolf
November 22, YR-1

DEPOSITION SUMMARY OF WALTER WILKINS

My name is Walt Wilkins. I am thirty-one years old and live at 1406 Logan Court in Nita City, Nita. I work as an after-hours trader in the Institutional Stock Market for Golden Investments, also in Nita City. As such my work day normally begins at 2:00 p.m. and goes until 9 p.m. I am single. One of my co-workers is Ken Brown. Ken and I have known each other since our college days at UCLA, where we both played on the tennis team. We both played singles, but we were best when playing together as doubles partners. We were good college players, but not good enough to turn professional. When we graduated from UCLA in YR-10, we both went to work for Golden Investments and have been employed there ever since.

I know about Ken's car accident through him and I have seen the effect it had on him. I came in early on April 20, YR-1, as a favor to Ken to cover his clients so he could catch a flight out of town that afternoon. I got in at about 2 p.m. Ken told me what I needed to know to cover him. He had plenty of time to get to the airport. His flight wasn't until 5 o'clock that night, but he had some errands to do before heading out to the airport. Ken likes to be early for flights; he likes to avoid the rush-hour traffic.

I first heard about the accident the next day. Ken called me at home that morning and asked me if I could pick him up and take him to his doctor's office. He told me he had been rear-ended by a guy at a stoplight and that he had been up most of the night at his hotel with his back and head bothering him. I was pleased to help him out. When I picked him up he looked terrible. He was walking all stooped over and it was obvious he was in a lot of pain. I asked him why he had gone on his trip, and he told me that he really didn't start to hurt until 2 a.m. when he woke up with a headache and his back in spasm.

Ken's life was much different for the rest of YR-1. With one exception, he and I did not play any tennis after the accident in YR-1. According to Ken, he may be allowed to play tennis in the near future. For most of YR-1 Ken was pretty depressed. His back really bothered him. He hardly ever went out socially, which we used to do regularly, and I know it affected his work performance. He was the number-one broker in our group at Golden in YR-2 and YR-3, and he slipped to next to last in YR-1. I know for a fact that his draw for YR-1 alone was $60,000 less than the year before. He has been making a comeback this year and is back near the top of the group.

Yes, there was a time after the accident that Ken tried to play tennis. One Saturday, I think it was in late June, Ken called me and said he had enough. He was feeling a little better and he wanted to play some tennis. I picked Ken up at his house and he seemed to be in good spirits. He said he had taken some muscle relaxants and felt pretty good. We went to the Nita Country Club where we both belong. We ended up playing a couple sets of tennis. Ken has always been a better player than me, relying on a big serve and great volley game. When we played that one time, he was about three-quarters speed. I toned my game down to meet his, but if I had wanted to I could have beaten him without his winning the game. His serve was nothing and his mobility was not great for him. I would be surprised if someone else described his play as anything else but mediocre, but I guess it's all about frame of reference. The way Ken was playing wasn't in the same league as his norm. After the game, we did drink a few beers,

Easy Tech: Cases and Materials on Courtroom Technology
© The National Institute for Trial Advocacy

which wasn't unusual. Ken said the beer tasted particularly good, as he hadn't been able to drink since the accident. I asked him if he should slow down on the beer (I think he had maybe four or five) but he said he wasn't worried because I was the designated driver.

We made plans to go out later that evening to get something to eat, but Ken called at the last minute and cancelled—said he had a headache. I know that he was out of work part of the next week with his back. At any rate, that was the last time I know of that Ken tried to play tennis. He is hoping to play again, I know, and he has seemed better physically around the office. I guess he's improving.

I have read this deposition, and it is complete and accurate.

Walter Wilkins

Walter Wilkins
November 23, YR-1

JURY INSTRUCTIONS

1. The Court will now instruct you about the law that governs this case. By your oath, you agreed to accept and follow these instructions and to apply them to the facts you find from the evidence. Any verdict in this case must be the unanimous decision of all jurors.

2. The plaintiff, Kenneth Brown, claims that the defendant, Robert Byrd, negligently injured him in a motor vehicle collision in Nita City on April 20, YR-1. The defendant denies that the collision caused the plaintiff any injury, and he also claims that the plaintiff negligently contributed to cause the collision and any injury the plaintiff sustained then.

3. Each party has the burden of proving his claim by a preponderance of the evidence, which is the greater weight of the evidence or the evidence that you find is more believable.

4. Negligence is the failure to exercise reasonable care, or the care that a reasonable person would exercise under the same or similar circumstances.

5. A driver must operate his vehicle in a manner that will permit him to stop without colliding with a vehicle ahead in his line of travel. A driver may enter an intersection when he faces a yellow or "caution" traffic control signal, but he has no duty to enter the intersection then if he reasonably believes that he will thereby endanger himself or others.

6. To reduce or eliminate the plaintiff's recovery for any injury, the defendant has the burden of proving that the plaintiff negligently contributed to cause that collision. In your interrogatory answers and verdict, you will determine whether the plaintiff negligently contributed to cause the collision and any injury he sustained then. If the plaintiff was more at fault than the defendant in causing the collision, your verdict should be for the defendant. If the defendant was as much or more at fault than the plaintiff in causing the collision, then the percent of fault for which the plaintiff was responsible shall reduce the plaintiff's recovery proportionately.

7. If your verdict is for the plaintiff, you should determine an amount which will fully and fairly compensate him for any injury or damage he proximately sustained in that collision, including compensation for any physical pain, emotional distress, or disability; the reasonable value of any medical care; and any loss of income he reasonably sustained. If you find with reasonable certainty that any injury he proximately sustained in that collision is permanent or will cause him future harm, you should also include an amount to compensate for that future pain, disability, or emotional distress.

Easy Tech: Cases and Materials on Courtroom Technology
© The National Institute for Trial Advocacy

IN THE UNITED STATES DISTRICT COURT
FOR THE DISTRICT OF NITA

KENNETH BROWN   )
)
    Plaintiff,   )   CIVIL NO. 2892
)
    vs.   )
)   SPECIAL VERDICT FORM
ROBERT BYRD   )
)
    Defendant.   )
_____)

SPECIAL VERDICT FORM

The jury must answer all of the questions, unless otherwise indicated. To understand what issues are being submitted to you, you may wish to read over the entire special verdict form before proceeding to answer the questions. Answer the questions in numerical order. Follow all directions carefully. <u>Each</u> answer requires the agreement of at least _____ jurors; however, the same _____ jurors need <u>not</u> agree on each answer.

QUESTION #1: Was the Defendant negligent?

           YES _____   NO _____

If your answer to Question #1 was "Yes", then please go on to answer Question #2. If your answer to Question #1 was "No", then the foreperson shall sign this document and summon the bailiff.

QUESTION #2: Was the negligence of Defendant a legal cause of Plaintiff's damages?

           YES _____   NO _____

If your answer to Question #2 was "YES", then please go on to answer Question #3. If your answer to Question #2 was "NO", then the foreperson shall sign this document and summon the bailiff.

QUESTION #3: Was Plaintiff contributorily negligent?

           YES _____   NO _____

If your answer to Question #3 was "YES", then please go on to answer Question #4. If your answer to Question #3 was "NO", then please skip Question #4 and Question #5 and go on to answer Question #6.

QUESTION #4: Was the contributory negligence of Plaintiff a legal cause of his damages?

YES _____   NO _____

If your answer to Question #4 was "YES", then please go on to answer Question #5. If your answer to Question #4 was "NO", then please skip Question #5 and go on to answer Question #6.

QUESTION #5: Please determine the respective negligence of Defendant and Plaintiff.

DEFENDANT   _____%

PLAINTIFF   _____%

TOTAL   __100__%

If you answered Question #5 by assigning 50% or less negligence to Plaintiff, then please go on to answer Question #6. If you answered Question #5 by assigning more than 50% negligence to Plaintiff, then the foreperson shall sign this document and summon the bailiff.

QUESTION #6: Without reduction for Plaintiff's contributory negligence, if any, what are his total damages:

SPECIAL DAMAGES $_____

GENERAL DAMAGES $_____

TOTAL $_____

_____
Foreperson

Easy Tech: Cases and Materials on Courtroom Technology
© The National Institute for Trial Advocacy

EXHIBIT 1

NITA CITY POLICE DEPARTMENT
Accident Report

1. Investigating Officer: D. Pierce		2. Badge No: 2157
3. Date: April 20, YR-1	4. Time: 3:40 p.m.	5. Place: Nita City
VEHICLE # 1		
6. Operator: Kenneth Brown	7. Address: 5 Scott Pl. N. C.	8. Vehicle Title #: G18M4443798
9. Year: YR-3	10. Make: Honda	11. Model: Sedan
12. Lic. Plate: GSB 356	13. State: Nita	14. Insurance: State Farm
15. Pol. #: 00528-24-2234	16. Towed: Driveable	17. Damage: Rear bumper and trunk
VEHICLE # 2		
6. Operator: Robert Byrd	7. Address: 104 E. Main, N. C.	8. Vehicle Title #: IP644W5772
9. Year: YR-1	10. Make: Volvo	11. Model: Sedan
12. Lic. Plate: KJM 044	13. State: Nita	14. Insurance: USAA
15. Pol. #: 3001-17750-1440	16. Towed: Driveable	17. Damage: Front fender
18. Principal Road: 12th Avenue	19. Speed Limit: 25	20. Intersecting Road: E. Main

21. Injuries:
None - minor accident

22. Narrative:
Interviewed both drivers. Vehicle #1 was traveling south on 12th Avenue. When he neared intersection of E. Main light was green. Light changed to yellow and #1 stopped short and was rear-ended by Vehicle #2. #2 appeared to be traveling within posted speed limit of 25 mph and to have his vehicle under control. #2 may have been following too close, but accident was made unavoidable by the sudden and unnecessary stop by #1. Note also that timing of yellow light was short as previously noted. In light of all of above—No Citations—Both vehicles driveable—No injuries.

23. Investigating Officer Signature: *David Pierce*	Date: 4/21/YR-1

EXHIBIT 2

5/7

Pain in back and neck starts after arrival in Chicago 4/20/Yr-1 Up all night with back and neck pain. Also terrible headache — doesn't respond to Tylenol or ibuprofen. Saw internist next day. Told pain is definitely from car wreck, though didn't seem hit that hard. Stayed home from work rest of week. Returned to work but not able to work full shift. Dr Gomes prescribes rest and ibuprofen. Informed if not better in couple of days try heat and massage treatment, maybe chiropractor. Pain still nagging in back, headaches are not as frequent by 5/5. Made appointment with Dr McCullough who has office in neighborhood, recommended by Arnie down the block. Treatment gives temporary relief from pain. Treatment schedule discussed. Pain not quite as bad but enough to notice today — unable to work full day.

5/10

Stretching a little in morning helps stiff back. Worked full day — pain distracting at work — by 6:00 back very painful. Called for McCullough appointment.

5/11

Back still bothering me — dull aching pain — had to leave work early. Set up regular treatments with Burmeister Clinic for heat, massage, hot bath therapy.

5/15

Burmeister helps but still stiff every morning — worked 6 hour days this week.

5/20

Sharp pain today reaching for a notebook at work — stays all day until I get to Burmeister.

EXHIBIT 2

5/30
Continuing dull pain in back —
missed two days work this week
first bad headache in two weeks.

6/8
Dull ache continues though a
little better - sharp pain, needed
massage, reaching for pan in
kitchen - still distracting at work

6/15
Had a pretty good week. Back
still hurts but not as bad.

6/25
Tried to play tennis today - big
mistake - back feels as bad as
right after accident.
See Dr. McCullough - ordered to
stay home and rest for week —
take vacation week.

7/4
Back to work - ok today for
first time — back sore tonight
really hurts at work - affects
concentration a lot.

8/10
Pain has been up and down, but
getting better - Burmeister appointments
seem to be helping. Less distracting
at work.

8/25
First bad day in couple of weeks.
Stayed in one position too long at desk,
got back spasms. OK after stretching.

10/15
Pretty good for almost a month —
every once in a while, like today,
I move too fast and get sharp
pain. Today lasted for a couple
hours and Tylenol didn't help.

10/17
Saw Dr. McCullough — he sees
good deal of improvement but
warns not to try too much.

11/20
Doc okays light tennis —
beginning with 20 minute
sessions.

EXHIBIT 3

GOLDEN INVESTMENTS
FINANCIAL ADVISORS
MEMBER
NITA STOCK EXCHANGE
16 BULL BOULEVARD
NITA CITY, NITA

March 31, YR-1

TO: Ken Brown

FROM: Alyssa Hoffman, Vice President

RE: Quarterly Review

For the period 1/1/YR-1 through 3/31/YR-1

Salary: $20,000

Commissions: $23,256

New Clients This Quarter: 11

As the above numbers show, there is some reason for concern in your performance during the first quarter of this year. Although there has been a small slowing the market, compared to the last quarter of YR-2, your commissions for this quarter are less than half for the last quarter of YR-2 when your commissions were $49,500. Similarly, while your client base was reduced by the death of your best investor, you have only 11 new customers in this quarter, when compared to the 31 new customers in the last quarter of YR-2. The comparison of the first quarter of this year with the first quarter of last year is also disappointing. Your commissions for the first quarter of YR-2 were $40,075 and new clients for that quarter were 23.

I am sure you share our disappointment concerning your performance, especially after your personal record year of YR-1. Ken, we all go through these droughts, especially after a big year. It's time to get back to work in earnest. With your talent, I expect that you can rescue this year if you just put your mind to it. I expect that we will see significant improvements in the next quarter.

If you need any assistance, please feel free to make an appointment with my personal assistant.

EXHIBIT 4

EXHIBIT 5

EXHIBIT 6

EXHIBIT 7

Easy Tech: Cases and Materials on Courtroom Technology
© The National Institute for Trial Advocacy

EXHIBIT 8

EXHIBIT 9

EXHIBIT 10

EXHIBIT 11

EXHIBIT 12

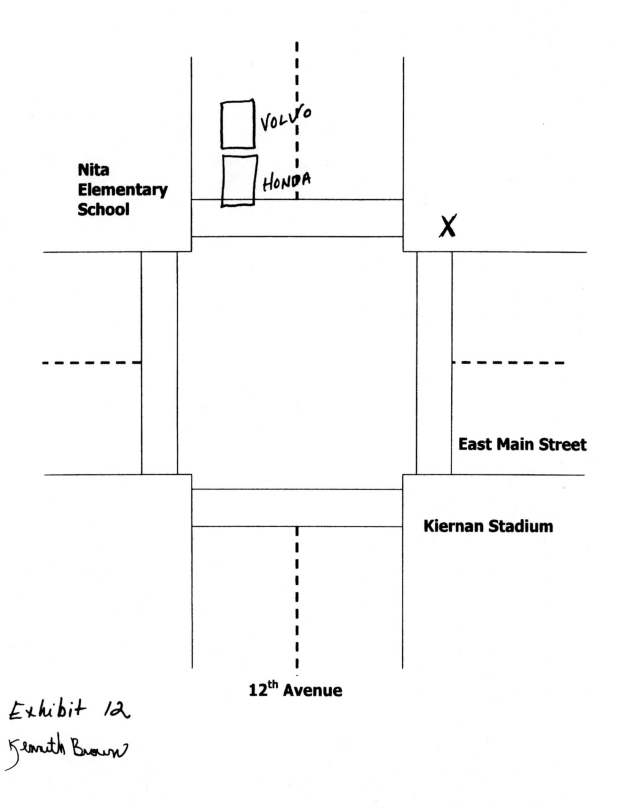

VOLVO

HONDA

**Nita
Elementary
School**

X

East Main Street

Kiernan Stadium

12ᵗʰ Avenue

Exhibit 12

Kenneth Brown

Easy Tech: Cases and Materials on Courtroom Technology
© The National Institute for Trial Advocacy

EXHIBIT 13

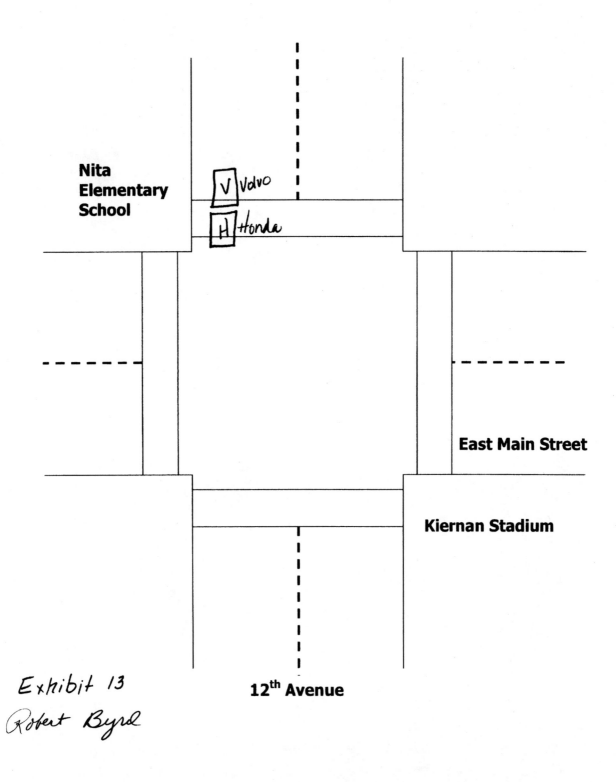

Nita
Elementary
School

V Volvo

H Honda

East Main Street

Kiernan Stadium

Exhibit 13
Robert Byrd

12ᵗʰ Avenue

EXHIBIT 14

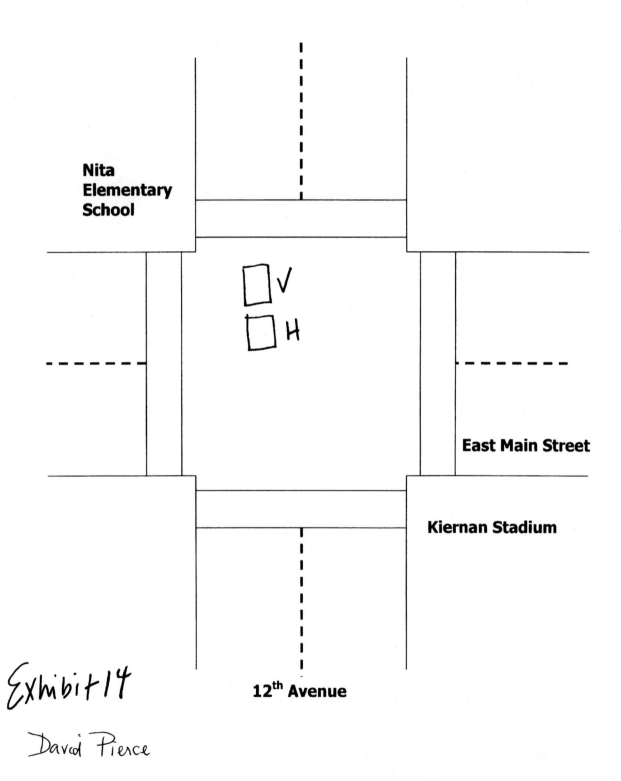

Nita Elementary School

East Main Street

Kiernan Stadium

12th Avenue

Exhibit 14

David Pierce

EXHIBIT 15

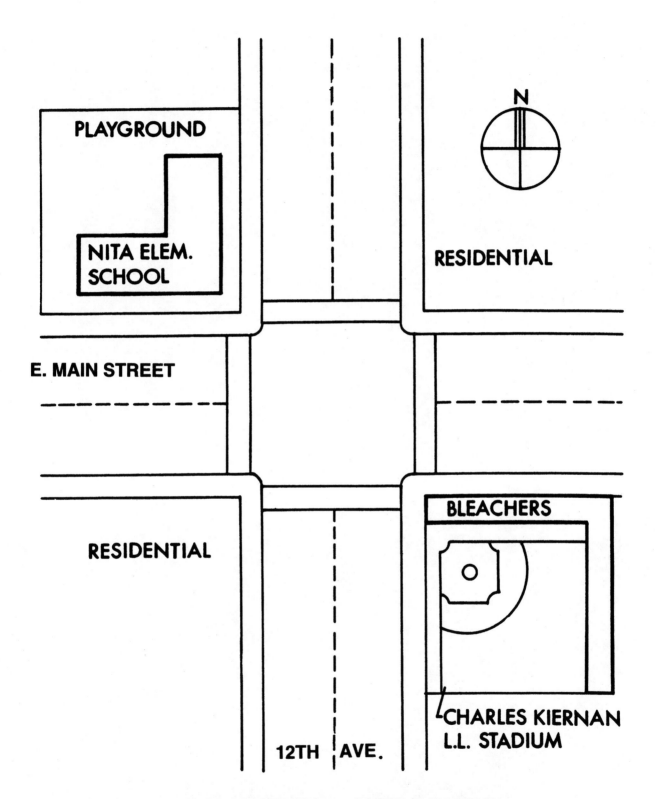

PLAYGROUND

NITA ELEM. SCHOOL

N

RESIDENTIAL

E. MAIN STREET

RESIDENTIAL

BLEACHERS

CHARLES KIERNAN L.L. STADIUM

12TH AVE.

INTERSECTION — 12TH & E. MAIN

EXHIBIT 16

Easy Tech: Cases and Materials on Courtroom Technology
© The National Institute for Trial Advocacy

EXHIBIT 17

Easy Tech: Cases and Materials on Courtroom Technology
© The National Institute for Trial Advocacy

EXHIBIT 18

9.   As a direct and proximate result of the negligence of Defendant, Plaintiff has

suffered severe injury, for which he must take pain medication, and pain and suffering.

Plaintiff has become unable to engage in strenuous work or exercise. Plaintiff has incurred

past and future medical and rehabilitative expenses, all in an amount which exceeds the tort

threshold set forth in Chapter 431 of the Nita Revised Statutes, and Plaintiff has suffered

mental and emotional distress, and has lost income and earning capacity.

WHEREFORE, Plaintiff prays that:

1.   He be given judgment against Defendant for special and general

       damages that may be proven at time of trial;

2.   He be awarded his costs and such other relief as this Court deems just

       and proper.

DATED: Nita City, Nita, July 15, YR-1.

_____
HARRIET COOPERMAN
Attorney for the Plaintiff

- 3 -

EXHIBIT 19

DR. DAVID McCULLOUGH
Board Certified Doctor of Chiropractic Medicine
421 Central Avenue, Nita City, Nita 00011

December 20, YR-1

Angeline Ferrari, Attorney at Law
1100 Central Bank Building
237 Market Street
Nita City, Nita 00012

Dear Ms. Ferrari:

In response to your request, I provide the following report about my care for your client, Kenneth Brown.

I have been Mr. Brown's health care provider for a back injury he received in an automobile accident in April of YR-1. In reviewing his medical records from his internist I note that he has been treated for various minor illnesses and provided annual physical examinations. He had no significant medical history or findings. He was a well developed, well nourished male with a very active athletic background, including competitive tennis and swimming activities.

HISTORY OF THIS INCIDENT: On the morning of April 21, YR-1 Patient telephoned his internist, Dr. Gomez, to request an emergency appointment that same day. Patient reported that on April 20 he had been the driver of a car that had been rear-ended, in which both vehicles sustained significant damage. At the moment of impact, Patient was leaning forward and looking to his left for possible approaching traffic, which made him more vulnerable to flexion-extension and torsion injury. Patient was wearing a combination lap and shoulder restraint, and the air bag did not deploy.

Patient said he was "shaken up" then but had no meaningful pain or restricted motion for several hours. Patient did not seek any medical attention that day and traveled several hours by plane to a business meeting. As is typical, there was no immediate discomfort to patient after collision. He became very uncomfortable that night and decided to come home to seek medical assistance the next morning, at which point, again as is typical, he was in quite a lot of pain.

At the time of Patient's first office visit to internist, Patient complained of a headache, severe pain in neck, and moderate pain in lower back. Upon examination, 40% restriction of neck rotation and flexion, and 30% limitation of low back flexion on straight leg raising (more on the left than the right) was noted. There was point tenderness and muscle spasm at or near C-6 and C-7 and at or near L-4 and L-5. A routine neurological examination was otherwise within normal limits with negative Babinski and Romberg tests, and bilaterally active and equal reflexes at the elbow, wrist, knee, and ankle. MRIs ordered—negative for herniation. Degeneration noted at L4–L5. Otherwise normal. Rest and ibuprofen for pain prescribed. Follow-up evaluation in ten days.

TREATMENT

Patient first seen on April 23, YR-1. Complete examination and chiropractic adjustment given. Progressive course of physical therapy recommended increasing from twice per week to three times per week over three months. Chiropractic adjustment schedule agreed upon. 3X/week until improvement. Confirmed diagnosis of Dr. Gomez. Burmeister's Physical Therapy Clinic later reported that Mr. Brown appeared for thirty physical therapy treatments there between May 5 and August 20, YR-1, which included deep heat, hot baths, massage, aquatherapy, and cervical traction.

When he returned to my office on May 1, YR-1, his condition had not improved. He had essentially the same complaints, and my findings were substantially the same. I began a regimen of Flexeril 10 mg. t.i.d. as a muscle relaxant, and Percocet 10 mg. p.r.n. for pain. I cautioned him that alcoholic beverages are contraindicated and potentially harmful while he uses these medications.

At my direction, he returned for forty-two further office visits, the most recent of which was last week on December 16. In July I prescribed a CT-Scan of his neck and back at NITA City Hospital, which the radiologist there interpreted as within normal limits. In August, I referred Mr. Brown to Dr. Phileas Fogg, a board certified orthopedist, who reported essentially the same findings I had made and ruled out a herniated nucleuous pulposus in the neck or back.

OPINION

Mr. Brown suffered a flexion-extension myofascial injury to his neck and low back, which produced moderate disability for at least three months and some continued disability thereafter. In my opinion, he will probably suffer some continued pain and disability indefinitely on extremes of motion, which might limit or preclude his participation in active athletic efforts. He has worked on stretching exercises and intends to try to play tennis. He has reported missing a number of days from his employment in the early course of his treatment. He may miss some days hereafter during normal exacerbations of his symptoms. He is to return to my office for further evaluation and adjustment as needed. I would expect Mr. Brown to continue such treatments for at least the next six to eight months.

My office manager advises me that my professional fees for treating this patient's injury have been $3,870.00. At your request, I reviewed Mr. Brown's bills from Burmeister's Clinic ($1,450.00), Nita City Hospital for CT-Scan ($400.00), Nita City Radiologists, Inc. ($150.00), and Dr. Fogg ($125.00). I found them all to be reasonable charges for necessary medical care. Please contact me if you require any further information.

Please remit $350.00 as my charge for this report.

Very truly yours,

Dr. David McCullough

Blank Slide **Slide 1**

Exhibit 1 **Slide 2**

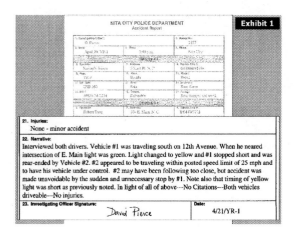

Exhibit 1 **Slide 3**

Exhibit 2 **Slide 4**

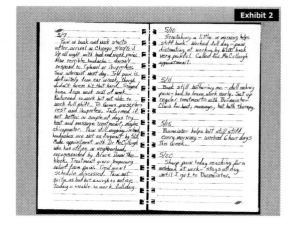

Exhibit 2 **Slide 5**

Exhibit 2 **Slide 6**

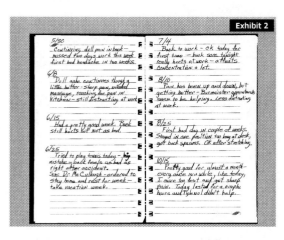

Easy Tech: Cases and Materials on Courtroom Technology
© The National Institute for Trial Advocacy

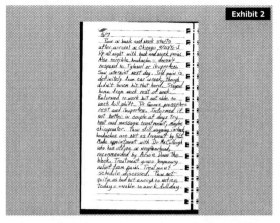

Exhibit 2   **Slide 7**

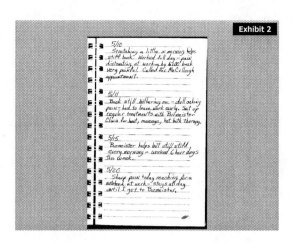

Exhibit 2   **Slide 8**

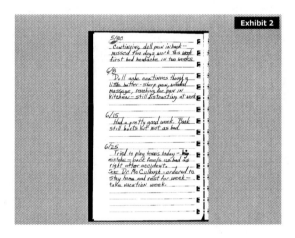

Exhibit 2   **Slide 9**

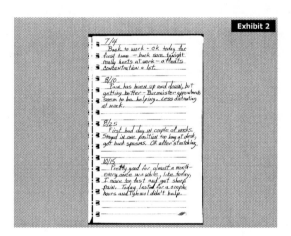

Exhibit 2   **Slide 10**

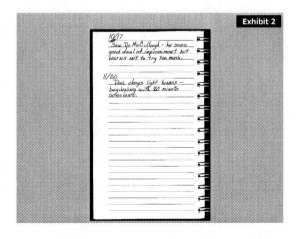

Exhibit 2   **Slide 11**

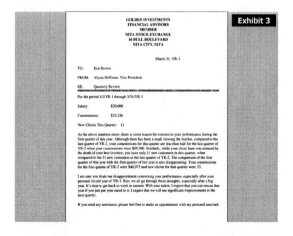

Exhibit 3   **Slide 12**

Easy Tech: Cases and Materials on Courtroom Technology
© The National Institute for Trial Advocacy

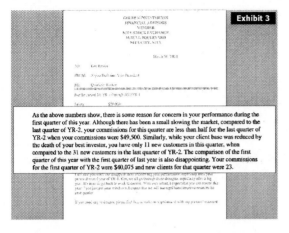

Exhibit 3   **Slide 13**

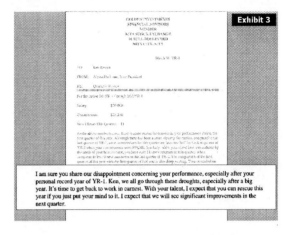

Exhibit 3   **Slide 14**

Exhibit 4   **Slide 15**

Exhibit 5   **Slide 16**

Exhibit 6   **Slide 17**

Exhibit 7   **Slide 18**

Easy Tech: Cases and Materials on Courtroom Technology
© The National Institute for Trial Advocacy

Exhibit 8   **Slide 19**

Exhibit 9   **Slide 20**

Exhibit 10   **Slide 21**

Exhibit 11   **Slide 22**

Two Months Later   **Slide 23**

Two Months Later   **Slide 24**

Easy Tech: Cases and Materials on Courtroom Technology
© The National Institute for Trial Advocacy

Two Months Later   **Slide 25**

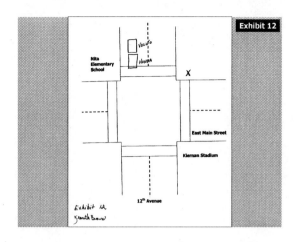

Exhibit 12   **Slide 26**

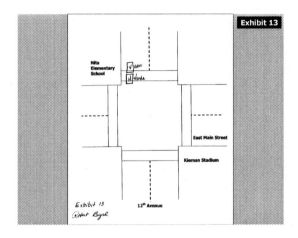

Exhibit 13   **Slide 27**

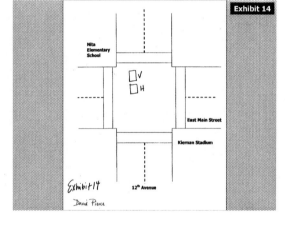

Exhibit 14   **Slide 28**

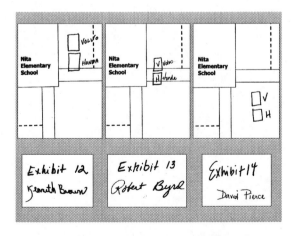

Exhibit 12, 13, 14   **Slide 29**

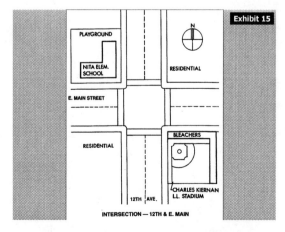

Exhibit 15   **Slide 30**

Easy Tech: Cases and Materials on Courtroom Technology
© The National Institute for Trial Advocacy

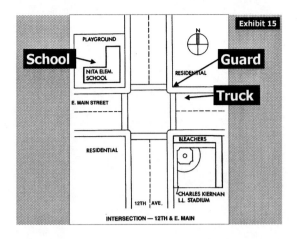

Exhibit 15   **Slide 31**

Exhibit 16   **Slide 32**

Exhibit 17   **Slide 33**

Exhibit 16 & 17   **Slide 34**

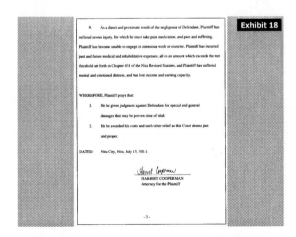

Exhibit 18   **Slide 35**

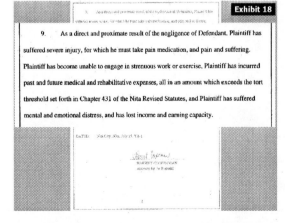

Exhibit 18   **Slide 36**

Easy Tech: Cases and Materials on Courtroom Technology
© The National Institute for Trial Advocacy

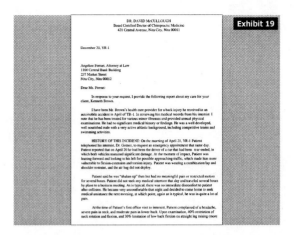

Exhibit 19

DR. DAVID McCULLOUGH
Board Certified Doctor of Chiropractic Medicine
421 Central Avenue, Nita City, Nita 00011

December 20, YR-1

Angeline Ferrari, Attorney at Law
1100 Central Bank Building
237 Market Street
Nita City, Nita 00012

Dear Ms. Ferrari:

In response to your request, I provide the following report about my care for your client, Kenneth Brown.

I have been Mr. Brown's health care provider for a back injury he received in an automobile accident in April of YR-1. In reviewing his medical records from his internist I note that he has been treated for various minor illnesses and provided annual physical examinations. He had no significant medical history or findings. He was a well developed, well nourished male with a very active athletic background, including competitive tennis and swimming activities.

HISTORY OF THIS INCIDENT: On the morning of April 21, YR-1 Patient telephoned his internist, Dr. Gomez, to request an emergency appointment that same day. Patient reported that on April 20 he had been the driver of a car that had been rear-ended, in which both vehicles sustained significant damage. At the moment of impact, Patient was leaning forward and looking to his left for possible approaching traffic, which made him more vulnerable to flexion-extension and torsion injury. Patient was wearing a combination lap and shoulder restraint, and the air bag did not deploy.

Patient said he was "shaken up" then but had no meaningful pain or restricted motion for several hours. Patient did not seek any medical attention that day and traveled several hours by plane to a business meeting. As is typical, there was no immediate discomfort to patient after collision. He became very uncomfortable that night and decided to come home to seek medical assistance the next morning, at which point, again as is typical, he was in quite a lot of pain.

At the time of Patient's first office visit to internist, Patient complained of a headache, severe pain in neck, and moderate pain in lower back. Upon examination, 40% restriction of neck rotation and flexion, and 30% limitation of low back flexion on straight leg raising (more

Exhibit 19   **Slide 37**

Exhibit 19

HISTORY OF THIS INCIDENT: On the morning of April 21, YR-1 Patient telephoned his internist, Dr. Gomez, to request an emergency appointment that same day. Patient reported that on April 20 he had been the driver of a car that had been rear-ended, in which both vehicles sustained significant damage. At the moment of impact, Patient was leaning forward and looking to his left for possible approaching traffic, which made him more vulnerable to flexion-extension and torsion injury. Patient was wearing a combination lap and shoulder restraint, and the air bag did not deploy.

Patient said he was "shaken up" then but had no meaningful pain or restricted motion for several hours. Patient did not seek any medical attention that day and traveled several hours by plane to a business meeting. As is typical, there was no immediate discomfort to patient after collision. He became very uncomfortable that night and decided to come home to seek medical assistance the next morning, at which point, again as is typical, he was in quite a lot of pain.

At the time of Patient's first office visit to internist, Patient complained of a headache, severe pain in neck, and moderate pain in lower back. Upon examination, 40% restriction of neck rotation and flexion, and 30% limitation of low back flexion on straight leg raising (more on the left than the right) was noted. There was point tenderness and muscle spasm at or near C-6 and C-7 and at or near L-4 and L-5. A routine neurological examination was otherwise within normal limits with negative Babinski and Romberg tests, and bilaterally active and equal reflexes at the elbow, wrist, knee, and ankle. MRIs ordered—negative for herniation. Degeneration noted at L4–L5. Otherwise normal. Rest and ibuprofen for pain prescribed. Follow-up evaluation in ten days.

Exhibit 19   **Slide 38**

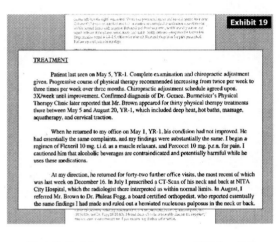

Exhibit 19

TREATMENT

Patient last seen on May 5, YR-1. Complete examination and chiropractic adjustment given. Progressive course of physical therapy recommended increasing from twice per week to three times per week over three months. Chiropractic adjustment schedule agreed upon. 3X/week until improvement. Confirmed diagnosis of Dr. Gomez. Burmeister's Physical Therapy Clinic later reported that Mr. Brown appeared for thirty physical therapy treatments there between May 5 and August 20, YR-1, which included deep heat, hot baths, massage, aquatherapy, and cervical traction.

When he returned to my office on May 1, YR-1, his condition had not improved. He had essentially the same complaints, and my findings were substantially the same. I began a regimen of Flexeril 10 mg. t.i.d. as a muscle relaxant, and Percocet 10 mg. p.r.n. for pain. I cautioned him that alcoholic beverages are contraindicated and potentially harmful while he uses these medications.

At my direction, he returned for forty-two further office visits, the most recent of which was last week on December 16. In July I prescribed a CT-Scan of his neck and back at NITA City Hospital, which the radiologist there interpreted as within normal limits. In August, I referred Mr. Brown to Dr. Phileas Fogg, a board certified orthopedist, who reported essentially the same findings I had made and ruled out a herniated nucleous pulposus in the neck or back.

Exhibit 19   **Slide 39**

Exhibit 19

TREATMENT

Patient last seen on May 5, YR-1. Complete examination and chiropractic adjustment given. Progressive course of physical therapy recommended increasing from twice per week to three times per week over three months. Chiropractic adjustment schedule agreed upon. 3X/week until improvement. Confirmed diagnosis of Dr. Gomez. Burmeister's Physical Therapy Clinic later reported that Mr. Brown appeared for thirty physical therapy treatments there between May 5 and August 20, YR-1, which included deep heat, hot baths, massage, aquatherapy, and cervical traction.

OPINION

Mr. Brown suffered a flexion-extension myofascial injury to his neck and low back, which produced moderate disability for at least three months and some continued disability thereafter. In my opinion, he will probably suffer some continued pain and disability indefinitely on extremes of motion, which might limit or preclude his participation in active athletic efforts. He has worked on stretching exercises and intends to try to play tennis. He has reported missing a number of days from his employment in the early course of his treatment. He may miss some days hereafter during normal exacerbations of his symptoms. He is to return to my office for further evaluation and adjustment as needed. I would expect Mr. Brown to continue such treatments for at least the next six to eight months.

My office manager advises me that my professional fees for treating this patient's injury have been $3,870.00. At your request, I reviewed Mr. Brown's bills from Burmeister's Clinic ($1,450.00), Nita City Hospital for CT-Scan ($400.00), Nita City Radiologists, Inc. ($150.00), and Dr. Fogg ($125.00). I found them all to be reasonable charges for necessary medical care. Please contact me if you require any further information.

Exhibit 19   **Slide 40**

Exhibit 19

Please count $350.00 as my charge for this report.

Very truly yours,

Dr. David McCullough

Exhibit 19   **Slide 41**

JURY INSTRUCTIONS

1.   The Court will now instruct you about the law that governs this case. By your oath, you agreed to accept and follow these instructions and to apply them to the facts you find from the evidence. Any verdict in this case must be the unanimous decision of all jurors.

2.   The plaintiff, Kenneth Brown, claims that the defendant, Robert Byrd, negligently injured him in a motor vehicle collision in Nita City on April 20, YR-1. The defendant denies that the collision caused the plaintiff any injury, and he also claims that the plaintiff negligently contributed to cause the collision and any injury the plaintiff sustained then.

3.   Each party has the burden of proving his claim by a preponderance of the evidence, which is the greater weight of the evidence or the evidence that you find more believable.

4.   Negligence is the failure to exercise reasonable care, or the care that a reasonable person would exercise under the same or similar circumstances.

5.   A driver must operate his vehicle in a manner that will permit him to stop without colliding with a vehicle ahead in his line of travel. A driver may enter an intersection when he faces a yellow or "caution" traffic control signal, but he has no duty to enter the intersection then if he reasonably believes that he will thereby endanger himself or others.

6.   To reduce or eliminate the plaintiff's recovery for any injury, the defendant has the burden of proving that the plaintiff negligently contributed to cause that collision. In your interrogatory answers and verdict, you will determine whether the plaintiff negligently contributed to cause the collision and any injury he sustained then. If the plaintiff was more at fault than the defendant in causing the collision, your verdict should be for the defendant. If the defendant was as much or more at fault than the plaintiff in causing the collision, then the percent of fault for which the plaintiff was responsible shall reduce the plaintiff's recovery proportionately.

7.   If your verdict is for the plaintiff, you should determine an amount which will fully and fairly compensate him for any injury or damage he proximately sustained in that collision, including compensation for any physical pain, emotional distress, or disability; the reasonable value of any medical care; and any loss of income he reasonably sustained. If you find with reasonable certainty that any injury he proximately sustained in that collision is permanent or will cause him future harm, you should also include an amount to compensate for that future pain, disability, or emotional distress.

Jury Instructions   **Slide 42**

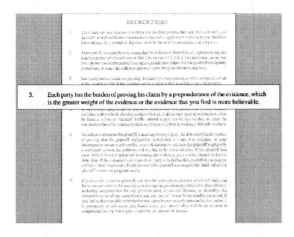

Jury Instruction 3 **Slide 43**

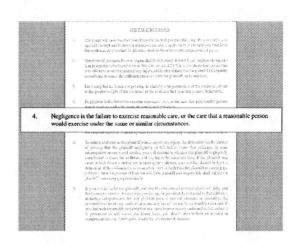

Jury Instruction 4 **Slide 44**

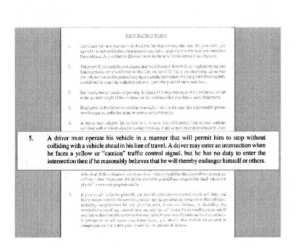

Jury Instruction 5 **Slide 45**

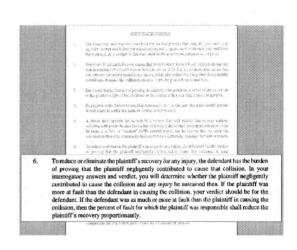

Jury Instruction 6 **Slide 46**

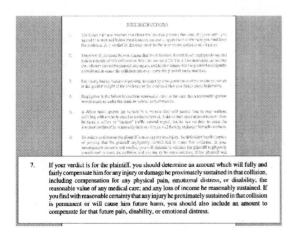

Jury Instruction 7 **Slide 47**

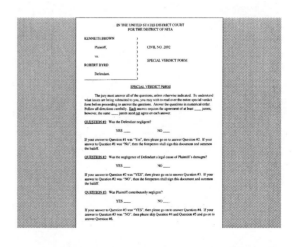

Verdict Form p. 1 **Slide 48**

Easy Tech: Cases and Materials on Courtroom Technology
© The National Institute for Trial Advocacy

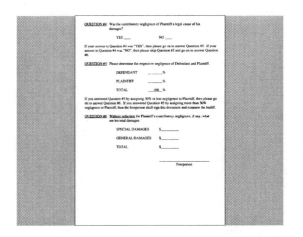

Verdict Form p. 2   **Slide 49**

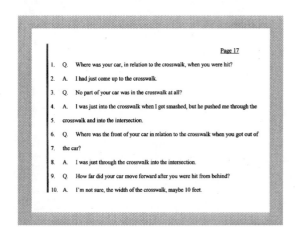

Brown p. 17, 1–10   **Slide 50**

Brown video   **Slide 51**

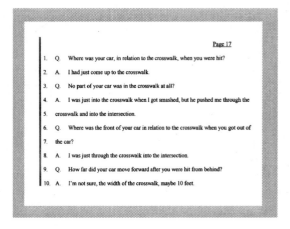

Brown Q & A reveal   **Slide 52**

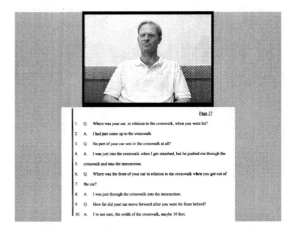

Brown video +   **Slide 53**

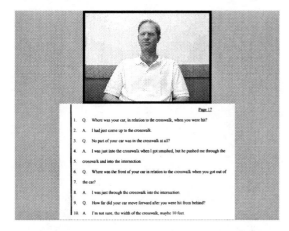

Brown video +   **Slide 54**

Easy Tech: Cases and Materials on Courtroom Technology
© The National Institute for Trial Advocacy

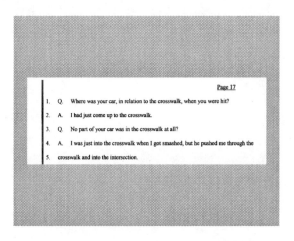

Brown p. 17, 1–5   **Slide 55**

Brown video   **Slide 56**

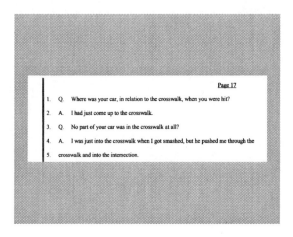

Brown Q & A reveal   **Slide 57**

Brown video +   **Slide 58**

Brown video +   **Slide 59**

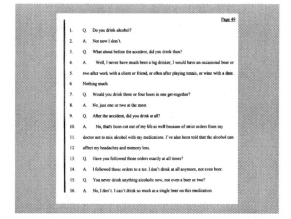

Brown p. 49, 1–16   **Slide 60**

Brown video   **Slide 61**

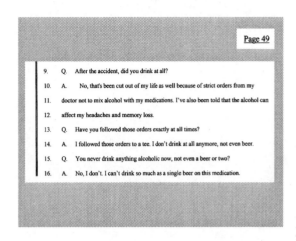

Brown p. 49, 9–16   **Slide 62**

Brown video   **Slide 63**

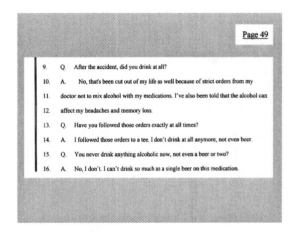

Brown Q & A reveal   **Slide 64**

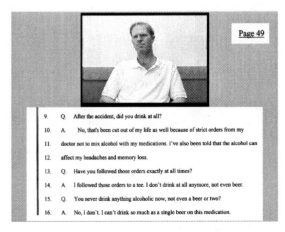

Brown video +   **Slide 65**

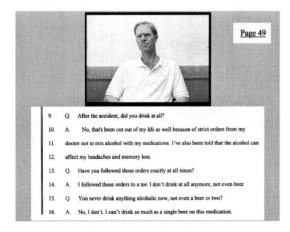

Brown video +   **Slide 66**

Easy Tech: Cases and Materials on Courtroom Technology
© The National Institute for Trial Advocacy

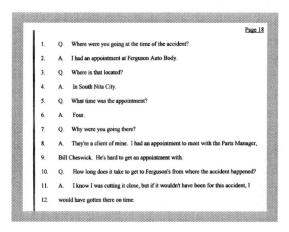

Byrd p. 18, 1–12   **Slide 67**

Byrd video   **Slide 68**

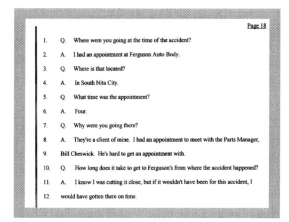

Byrd Q & A reveal   **Slide 69**

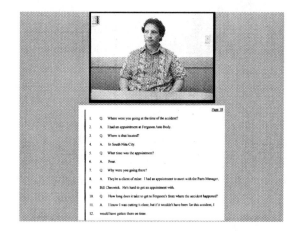

Byrd video +   **Slide 70**

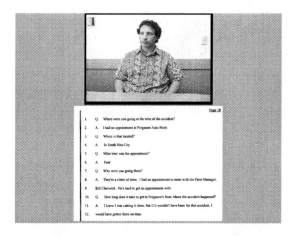

Byrd video +   **Slide 71**

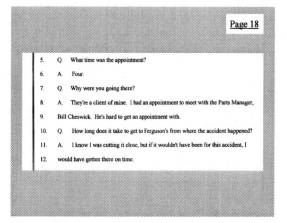

Byrd p. 18, 5–12   **Slide 72**

Byrd video   **Slide 73**

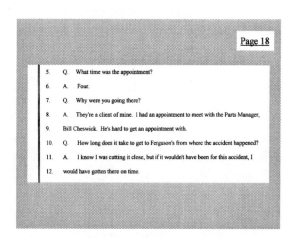

Byrd Q & A reveal   **Slide 74**

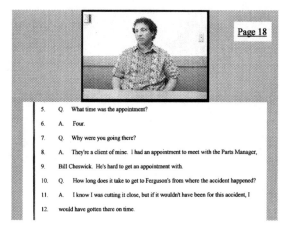

Byrd video +   **Slide 75**

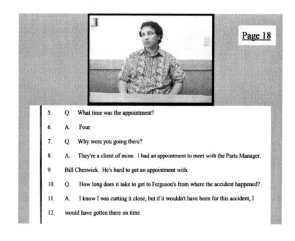

Byrd video +   **Slide 76**

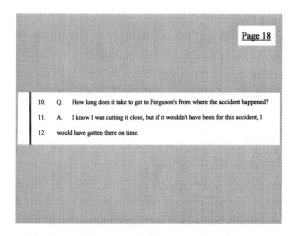

Byrd p. 18, 10–12   **Slide 77**

Byrd video   **Slide 78**

Easy Tech: Cases and Materials on Courtroom Technology
© The National Institute for Trial Advocacy

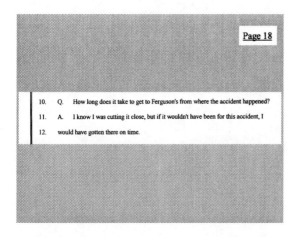

Page 18

10. Q. How long does it take to get to Ferguson's from where the accident happened?
11. A. I know I was cutting it close, but if it wouldn't have been for this accident, I
12. would have gotten there on time.

Q & A reveal   **Slide 79**

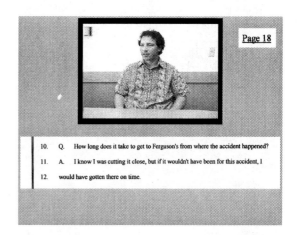

Page 18

10. Q. How long does it take to get to Ferguson's from where the accident happened?
11. A. I know I was cutting it close, but if it wouldn't have been for this accident, I
12. would have gotten there on time.

Byrd video +   **Slide 80**

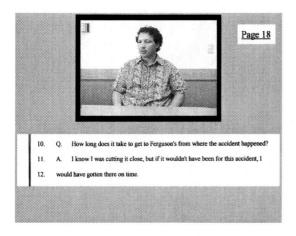

Page 18

10. Q. How long does it take to get to Ferguson's from where the accident happened?
11. A. I know I was cutting it close, but if it wouldn't have been for this accident, I
12. would have gotten there on time.

Byrd video +   **Slide 81**

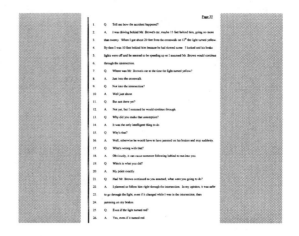

Byrd p. 35, 1–16   **Slide 82**

Byrd video   **Slide 83**

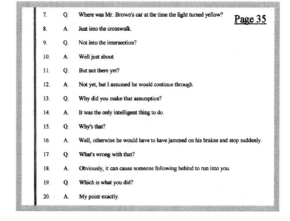

Page 35

7. Q. Where was Mr. Brown's car at the time the light turned yellow?
8. A. Just into the crosswalk.
9. Q. Not into the intersection?
10. A. Well just about.
11. Q. But not there yet?
12. A. Not yet, but I assumed he would continue through.
13. Q. Why did you make that assumption?
14. A. It was the only intelligent thing to do.
15. Q. Why's that?
16. A. Well, otherwise he would have to have jammed on his brakes and stop suddenly.
17. Q. What's wrong with that?
18. A. Obviously, it can cause someone following behind to run into you.
19. Q. Which is what you did?
20. A. My point exactly.

Byrd p. 35, 7–20   **Slide 84**

Byrd video   **Slide 85**

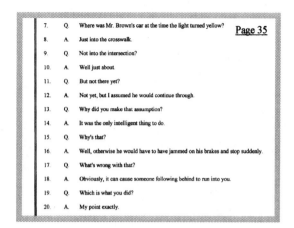

7. Q. Where was Mr. Brown's car at the time the light turned yellow?   Page 35
8. A. Just into the crosswalk.
9. Q. Not into the intersection?
10. A. Well just about.
11. Q. But not there yet?
12. A. Not yet, but I assumed he would continue through.
13. Q. Why did you make that assumption?
14. A. It was the only intelligent thing to do.
15. Q. Why's that?
16. A. Well, otherwise he would have to have jammed on his brakes and stop suddenly.
17. Q. What's wrong with that?
18. A. Obviously, it can cause someone following behind to run into you.
19. Q. Which is what you did?
20. A. My point exactly.

Byrd Q & A reveal   **Slide 86**

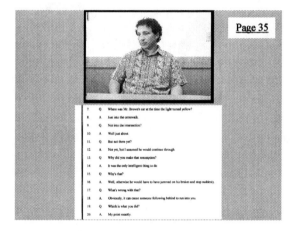

Byrd video +   **Slide 87**

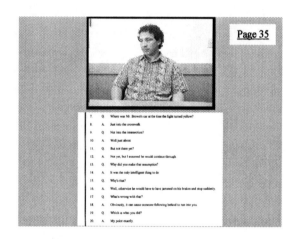

Byrd video +   **Slide 88**

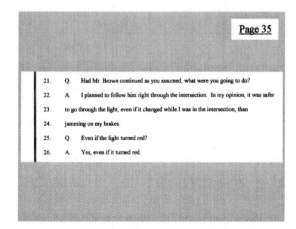

Page 35

21. Q. Had Mr. Brown continued as you assumed, what were you going to do?
22. A. I planned to follow him right through the intersection. In my opinion, it was safer
23.   to go through the light, even if it changed while I was in the intersection, than
24.   jamming on my brakes.
25. Q. Even if the light turned red?
26. A. Yes, even if it turned red.

Byrd p. 35, 21–26   **Slide 89**

Byrd video   **Slide 90**

Easy Tech: Cases and Materials on Courtroom Technology
© The National Institute for Trial Advocacy

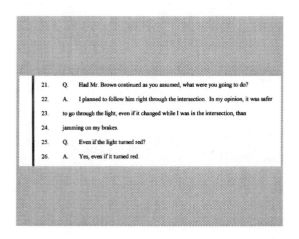

Byrd Q & A reveal   **Slide 91**

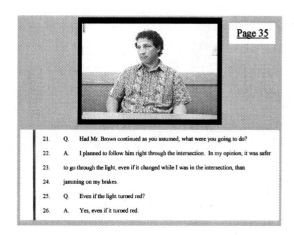

Byrd video +   **Slide 92**

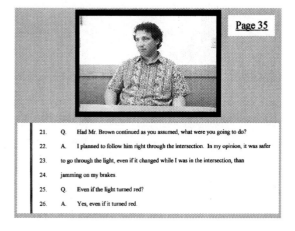

Byrd video +   **Slide 93**

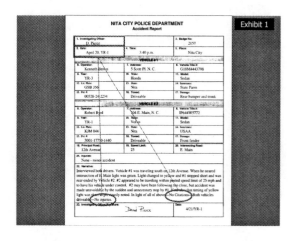

Exhibit 1   **Slide 94**

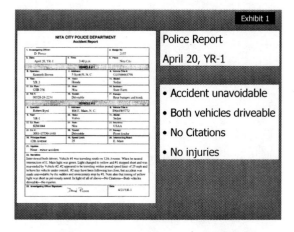

Exhibit 1   **Slide 95**

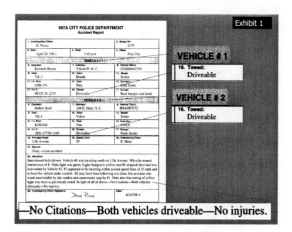

Exhibit 1   **Slide 96**

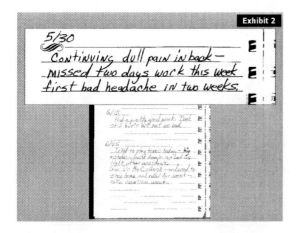

Exhibit 2   **Slide 97**

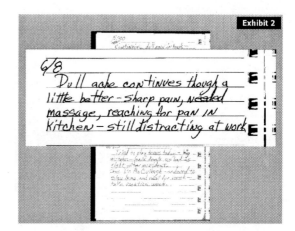

Exhibit 2   **Slide 98**

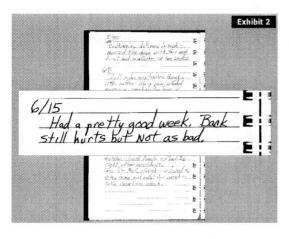

Exhibit 2   **Slide 99**

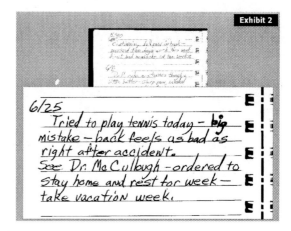

Exhibit 2   **Slide 100**

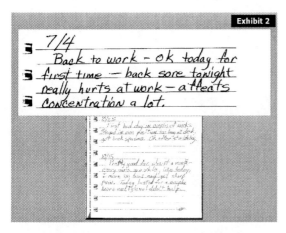

Exhibit 2   **Slide 101**

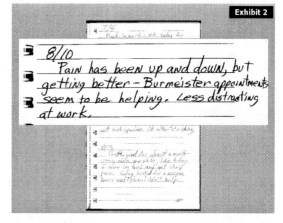

Exhibit 3   **Slide 102**

Easy Tech: Cases and Materials on Courtroom Technology
© The National Institute for Trial Advocacy

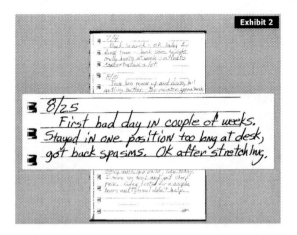

Exhibit 2 **Slide 103**

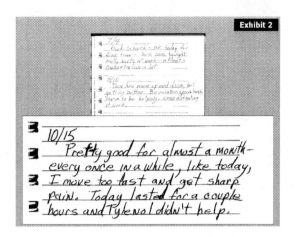

Exhibit 2 **Slide 104**

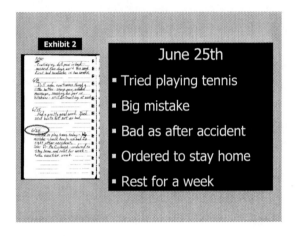

Exhibit 2 **Slide 105**

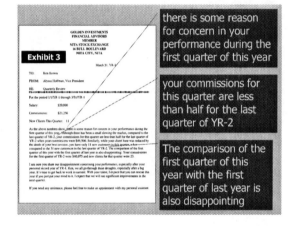

Exhibit 3 **Slide 106**

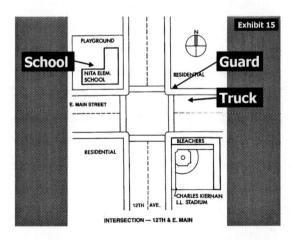

Exhibit 15 **Slide 107**

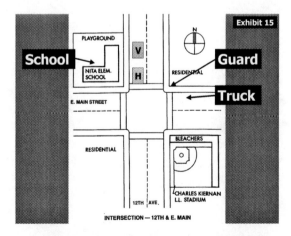

Ex. 15, PL version 1 **Slide 108**

Easy Tech: Cases and Materials on Courtroom Technology
© The National Institute for Trial Advocacy

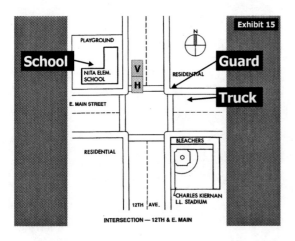

Ex. 15, PL version 2   **Slide 109**

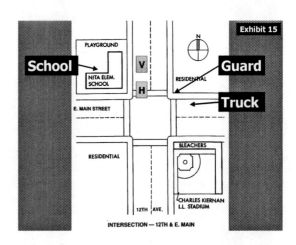

Ex. 15, DF version 1   **Slide 110**

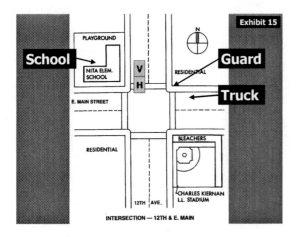

Ex. 15, PL version 2   **Slide 111**

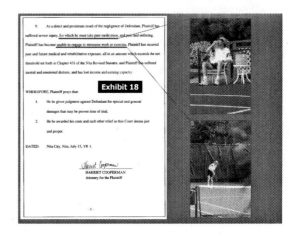

Exhibit 18   **Slide 112**

Hard-earned lesson

June 25th	July 4th
Tried to play tennis	Worked
Big mistake	Back sore
Bad as after 4/20	Really hurts
Home for a week	Can't concentrate

Hard-earned lesson   **Slide 113**

Defendant Byrd

- Light turns yellow
  - Assumes car going thru
  - Plans to go thru himself
  - Looks left and right for traffic
- Car in front stops
- Byrd doesn't stop
- Slams into rear of car in front

Defendant Byrd   **Slide 114**

Defendant Byrd

- 4 p.m. appointment
- "Cutting it close"
- School zone
- Looking at:
    - Kids on NW corner
    - Guard on NE corner
    - Kids at ice cream truck

Defendant Byrd　　　　**Slide 115**

Defendant Byrd

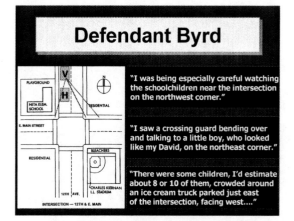

"I was being especially careful watching the schoolchildren near the intersection on the northwest corner."

"I saw a crossing guard bending over and talking to a little boy, who looked like my David, on the northeast corner."

"There were some children, I'd estimate about 8 or 10 of them, crowded around an ice cream truck parked just east of the intersection, facing west...."

Defendant Byrd　　　　**Slide 116**

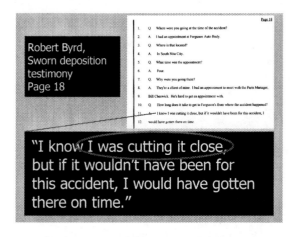

Robert Byrd, Sworn deposition testimony Page 18

"I know I was cutting it close, but if it wouldn't have been for this accident, I would have gotten there on time."

Byrd p. 18 callout　　　　**Slide 117**

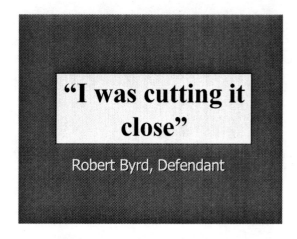

"I was cutting it close"

Robert Byrd, Defendant

Cutting it close　　　　**Slide 118**

The Accident

- ✓ 12th Avenue before Main Street
- ✓ Following Brown's Honda, 20 mph
- ✓ Car at crosswalk, light turns yellow
- ✓ Brown jams brakes, in intersection

The Accident　　　　**Slide 119**

The Injury

- ✓ Both cars drivable, damage minor
- ✓ Officer concludes: "No injuries"
- ✓ 2 months later Brown plays tennis
- ✓ No sign of injury playing tennis

The Injury　　　　**Slide 120**

-327-
Easy Tech: Cases and Materials on Courtroom Technology
© The National Institute for Trial Advocacy

Sudden stop **Slide 121**

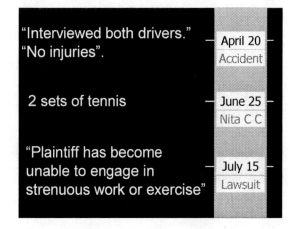

Time line **Slide 122**

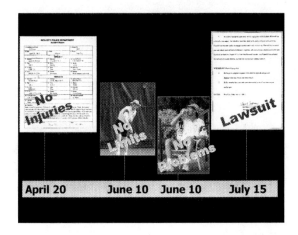

Time line **Slide 123**

Plaintiff claims **Slide 124**

"there is some reason for concern in your performance"			
3 month period	January to March, YR-2	October to Dec., YR-2	January to March, YR-1
Commissions	$40,075	$49,500	$23,256
New customers	23	31	11

Reason for concern **Slide 125**

Brown's quarterly reviews			
3 month period	January to March, YR-2	October to Dec., YR-2	January to March, YR-1
Commissions	$40,075	$49,500	$23,256
New customers	23	31	11

Brown's review **Slide 126**

PROBLEM 1
(Exhibits: Diary)

For the Plaintiff, introduce Brown's diary (Exhibit 2) in evidence. When showing the proposed exhibit to the court, counsel, and the witness for foundational purposes, utilize the electronic form of the exhibit. Assume the judge can prevent the jury from viewing the exhibit until it is introduced in evidence.

For the Defendant, oppose the offer.

PROBLEM 2
(Exhibits: Evaluation)

For the Defendant, introduce Brown's quarterly work evaluation (Exhibit 3) in evidence. Assume that the exhibit was produced electronically pursuant to Defendant's Request for Production of Documents. When showing the proposed exhibit to the court, opposing counsel, and the witness for foundational purposes, utilize the electronic form of the exhibit. Assume the judge can prevent the jury from viewing the exhibit until it is introduced in evidence.

For the Plaintiff, oppose the offer.

PROBLEM 3
(Exhibits: Photos)

For the Defendant, introduce the photos of Brown playing tennis (Exhibits 4–7) in evidence and make use of them in the direct examination of David Randolf, utilizing the evidence camera as the display device.

For the Plaintiff, oppose the offer and use.

PROBLEM 4
(Exhibits: Photos)

For the Plaintiff, use the photos of Brown playing tennis (Exhibits 4–7) which have already been admitted in evidence in the cross-examination of David Randolf, utilizing the evidence camera as the display device.

For the Defendant, oppose the use.

Easy Tech: Cases and Materials in Courtroom Technology
© The National Institute for Trial Advocacy

PROBLEM 5
(Direct examination with illustrative aid: Diagram)

For the Plaintiff, conduct the direct examination of Brown concerning how the accident occurred utilizing the diagram (Exhibit 15) as an illustrative aid.

Part A: Use the evidence camera and marking pen as the display device during your examination.

Part B: Use the computer and telestrator as the display device during your examination.

For the Defendant, oppose the offer and use in Parts A and B

PROBLEM 6
(Direct examination with illustrative aid: Diagram)

For the Defendant, conduct the direct examination of Byrd regarding how the accident occurred utilizing the diagram (Exhibit 15) as an illustrative aid.

Part A: Use the evidence camera and marking pen as the display device during your examination.

Part B: Use the computer and telestrator as the display device during your examination.

For the Plaintiff, oppose the offer and use in Parts A and B.

PROBLEM 7
(Direct examination with exhibit: Diary)

For the Plaintiff, conduct the direct examination of Ken Brown regarding his pain and suffering utilizing his diary (Exhibit 2). Be prepared to respond to objections regarding the use of the exhibit.

Part A: Use the evidence camera and marking pen as the display device during your examination.

Part B: Use the computer and telestrator as the display device during your examination.

Part C: Use the computer slide show with callouts and bullet points (PowerPoint slides 4–11) as the display device during your examination.

For the Defendant, oppose the offer and use in Parts A, B, and C.

Easy Tech: Cases and Materials in Courtroom Technology
© The National Institute for Trial Advocacy

PROBLEM 8
(Cross-examination with exhibit: Evaluation)

For the Defendant, conduct the cross-examination of Ken Brown regarding his wage loss claim utilizing his quarterly work evaluation (Exhibit 3). Be prepared to respond to objections regarding the use of this exhibit.

Part A: Use the evidence camera and marking pen as the display device during your examination.

Part B: Use the computer and telestrator as the display device during your examination.

Part C: Use the computer slide show with callouts and bullet points (PowerPoint slides 12–14) as the display device during your examination.

For the Plaintiff, oppose the offer and use in Parts A, B, and C.

PROBLEM 9
(Impeachment using transcript/video excerpt: Brown)

On direct examination, the Plaintiff has testified to the following: "I stopped before I got to the crosswalk. My car wasn't in the crosswalk until after he smashed into me."

For the Defendant, conduct the impeachment of Brown.

Part A: Conduct the impeachment of Brown utilizing whatever portions you choose of the transcript of his testimony that appears in this volume.

Part B: Conduct the impeachment of Brown utilizing whatever portions you choose of the videotape of his deposition testimony which appear in the PowerPoint slide show on your CD.

Part C: Conduct the impeachment of Brown utilizing whatever portions you choose of the videotape of his deposition testimony with the scrolling written transcript appearing beneath it which appear in the PowerPoint slide show on your CD.

For the Plaintiff, oppose the impeachment and the use of exhibits in Parts A, B, and C.

Easy Tech: Cases and Materials in Courtroom Technology
© The National Institute for Trial Advocacy

PROBLEM 10
(Impeachment using transcript/video excerpt: Byrd)

On direct examination, the Defendant has testified to the following: "At the time of the accident, I was headed for an appointment at Ferguson Auto Body. I was going slowly. I wasn't in any rush."

For Plaintiff, conduct the impeachment of Byrd.

Part A: Conduct the impeachment of Byrd utilizing whatever portions you choose of the transcript of his testimony that appears in this volume.

Part B: Conduct the impeachment of Byrd utilizing whatever portions you choose of the videotape of his deposition testimony which appear in the PowerPoint slide show on your CD.

Part C: Conduct the impeachment of Byrd utilizing whatever portions you choose of the videotape of his deposition testimony with the scrolling written transcript appearing beneath it which appear in the PowerPoint slide show on your CD.

For the Plaintiff, oppose the impeachment and the use of exhibits in Parts A, B, and C.

For the purposes of Problems 11–14, you need not go through a formal foundation before exhibits can be offered in evidence. Simply make the offer and be prepared to argue admissibility based on the facts in the file should there be an objection.

PROBLEM 11
(Direct and cross-examination: Brown)

For the Plaintiff, conduct the direct examination of Ken Brown utilizing the exhibits and illustrative aids in the file of your own choosing.

For the Defendant, conduct the cross-examination of Brown utilizing the exhibits and illustrative aids in the file of your own choosing.

PROBLEM 12
(Direct and cross-examination: Byrd)

For the Defendant, conduct the direct examination of Bob Byrd utilizing the exhibits and illustrative aids in the file of your own choosing.

For the Plaintiff, conduct the cross-examination of Byrd utilizing the exhibits and illustrative aids in the file of your own choosing.

Easy Tech: Cases and Materials in Courtroom Technology
© The National Institute for Trial Advocacy

PROBLEM 13
(Direct and cross-examination: Wilkins)

For the Plaintiff, conduct the direct examination of Walter Wilkins utilizing the exhibits and illustrative aids in the file of your own choosing.

For the Defendant, conduct the cross-examination of Wilkins utilizing the exhibits and illustrative aids in the file of your own choosing.

PROBLEM 14
(Direct and cross-examination: Randolf)

For the Defendant, conduct the direct examination of David Randolf utilizing the exhibits and illustrative aids in the file of your own choosing.

For the Plaintiff, conduct the cross-examination of Randolf utilizing the exhibits and illustrative aids in the file of your own choosing.

PROBLEM 15
(Opening statement)

Prepare a ten-minute portion of the opening statement for your client in the case of Brown v. Byrd. Assume the trial judge has ruled that you may utilize any evidentiary exhibit (in hard copy or in electronic form, displayed in the manner of your own choosing) in the case, during the opening statement. Any illustrative aids, either from the file or of your own creation, must be shown to your opponent, who will have an opportunity to make objections for the judge's ruling. A brief hearing on the use of illustrative aids will be conducted. The hearing does not count toward the ten-minute portion of the opening statement assigned by the problem.

PROBLEM 16
(Closing argument)

Prepare a fifteen-minute portion of the closing argument for your client in the case of Brown v. Byrd. In performing this exercise, you may utilize any admissible evidentiary exhibit. In addition, you must use *at least* one illustrative aid from the file or of your own creation. The evidentiary exhibits and illustrative aids may be displayed in any form, utilizing the display device of your choosing. The choice and use of exhibits and illustrative aids will be one of the points of critique for this exercise.

Easy Tech: Cases and Materials in Courtroom Technology
© The National Institute for Trial Advocacy